WOMEN IN THE
MIDDLE EAST

WOMEN IN THE MIDDLE EAST

**Magida Salman ★ Hamida Kazi ★ Nira Yuval-Davis
Laila al-Hamdani ★ Selma Botman ★ Debbie Lerman**

khamsin

Zed Books Ltd.
London and New Jersey

Women in the Middle East was first published by Zed Books Ltd., 57 Caledonian Road, London N1 9BU, UK, and 171 First Avenue, Atlantic Highlands, New Jersey 07716, USA, in 1987.

Copyright © Khamsin 1987

Typeset by Boldface, 17a Clerkenwell Road, London EC1M 5RD
Cover design Adrian Yeeles (Artworkers)
Cover photograph Torla Evans
Printed and bound in the UK by Cox and Wyman Ltd

British Library Cataloguing in Publication Data

Women in the Middle East.
   1. Women – Middle East – Social conditions
   I. Khamsin Collective
   305.4'2'0956   HQ1276.5

   ISBN 0-86232-674-5
   ISBN 0-86232-675-3 Pbk

CONTENTS

Introduction

The position of women in the Middle East, and their role in the various processes and struggles for social and political change which are taking place in the area, are of crucial importance. This is so, both when we try to understand the societies of which they are a part, as well as when we consider general issues of women's struggles.

This is the second time *Khamsin* dwells on the subject of women. *Khamsin* no. 6, which included some systematic attempts to examine these issues in the Arab world and in Israel, is now out of print, although demand for it continues. Rather than reprinting it, we decided to dedicate another issue to the subject, updating and deepening some of the aspects of the analysis which we started then. We hope to continue this work in future issues.

The first article in the issue, by Magida Salman, a Lebanese feminist, attempts to describe and analyse some of the most general characteristics of gender relations in the Middle East as they have been constructed by the Muslim view of women's 'nature'. Only by understanding this basic perspective, hegemonic in the Arab society, can we appreciate the nature of the task which has confronted Arab women (and men) who have struggled to change this state of affairs.

The second article in this issue, by Selma Botman, looks at the political role played by Egyptian women (in the years 1939-52) who had to contend with this very reality. The article, however, written by an Egyptian feminist (and graduate student at Harvard University) goes further than that and points out some of the inherent practical, not to mention ideological, contradictions that have occurred between specific struggles for the change in the position of women and the general radical nationalist movement that took over political power in Egypt in the 1950s.

The relationship between women's struggle and the struggle for national liberation is the focus of the next article, by Hamida Kazi, an Indian feminist who studied the condition of Palestinian women in the West Bank for her Ph.D. thesis at the LSE (University of London).

Some Palestinian women have paid a high price for their participation in the Palestinian liberation struggle. Laila al-Hamdani, a Palestinian socialist, was arrested and put in an Israeli prison for three years for having been a political activist while a student in Bir-Zeit University. She describes, for the first time, the daily lives of Palestinian women political prisoners, their self-organization and their encounters with Israeli Jews–both as ambivalent fellow prisoners and as prison authorities.

An endemic question in the Israeli feminist movement, which has caused deep rifts at general feminist annual conferences, is the question of the co-operation between Israeli-Jewish and Palestinian-Arab (both those who are Israeli citizens and those who live in the Occupied Territories) feminists. Debbie Lerman, an Israeli Jewish socialist-feminist has written a short piece to open the debate on why there has not been more co-operation between women of both nationalities, and on how to promote a common struggle.

The last article in the issue is written by Nira Yuval-Davis, an Israeli socialist-feminist sociologist. In her article she substantiates some of the claims made in the previous piece on the constraints on the position of Israeli women as a result of the nature of Israel as a Zionist state. She examines the role of Israeli Jewish women as reproducers of the national collectivity and concentrates especially on the 'demographic race' which is often seen as vital to the survival of Israel as the Jewish state.

As our readers will note, *Khamsin* is now published by Zed Books. It will now appear as a series rather than a periodical (note the change from an ISSN number to an ISBN number). There is no change in the editorial structure and policy, but we do hope for an improved distribution. We call upon our readers to support us in that, as well as sending us relevant articles to consider for publication.

Magida Salman

THE ARAB WOMAN

NOTWITHSTANDING HER CONDITION, whether as a peasant in Algeria, a doctor in Cairo, or a secretary in Beirut, a student in Baghdad, a worker in Syria, or veiled in a Harem in Saudi Arabia, the Arab woman shares with her sisters a common fate: a life of renunciation, of captivity, during which she will have to atone for her sin of having been born a woman in a hyper-male society where the ever-present feminine remains synonymous with shame and threat.

To begin with, her birth is already perceived as an occasion for mourning rather than for festivities. She is received in an atmosphere of barely suppressed disappointment. They hoped for a boy. Her coming will bring opprobrium on her mother, a shock to her father: 'Men beget men,' we always say in our culture; 'She has given birth to a girl, he has *produced* a boy,' they proclaim, totally ignorant of the laws of reproduction.

What happens on the day when the baby girl leaves her mother's womb is only a foretaste. It is the beginning of a life to be endured as a 'blameful condition' which will be continuously punctuated by steady and heavy repression and intolerance towards the social and economic changes deriving from our 'modern times'. A repression which may on the one hand end up in a death sentence, when the honour of the males is discredited by the non-virginity of their daughter, or, on the other hand, more often, a kind of life sentence in jail–behind a dark veil, behind the thick walls of the family house where the men act as jailors.

The world of childhood is always portrayed as an enchanted and smiling one in fairy stories and novels. However, the Arab girl's childhood is all too brief; it mirrors and prepares all too soon for the negative and submissive role which is assigned to the Arab woman, to endure men without really knowing them or being understood by them.

The Arab family where the fate of women is being decided and unfolds, remains, essentially, a Muslim family. Islam and its laws, its customs, its intrusions in the minutest details in human behaviour, have not been vanquished by the influence of imperialism or the defeat of imperialism. On the contrary. Due to a triumphant anachronism, Islam remains the basis and the *dynamic* force of the Arab family. Today, there is no Arab country (except Lebanon due to its religious-ethnic formation) where the constitution does not mention Islam as a State religion. There is no Arab country (except Tunisia and South Yemen) where the laws on the status of the family are not faithful to the letter, or directly inspired by, the laws of the Shari'a (Islamic law).

Adolescence

THE ADOLESCENCE of the young Arab girl is neither acknowledged nor lived as such in the Arab-Islamic tradition: the family feels perpetually threatened by the presence of a girl growing out of childhood and not married. The arrival of menstruation is accompanied by the haunting problem of the virginity–the honour of the girl which must from then on be supervised, hidden and controlled.

Puberty constitutes the end of childhood and the beginning of seclusion in the narrow world of the feminine space: a world of Harem, even if the latter does not exist in its traditional forms. It is enough to take a quick look into the Arab coffee houses, where only the males gather in large numbers, or to walk, any evening, in the districts catering for leisure and entertainments, in order to grasp the dimensions of that segregation which has created two worlds impervious to each other and which keeps young men and young women apart in the Arab world. The consequences of this separation can be seen in women as well as in men.

In her autobiography, entitled *O My Muslim Sisters Cry*, Zubeida Bittari tells of the sufferings and the shock she endured when, after her first menstruation, her Algerian parents, already modern in their way of life, took her out of school forcibly and obliged her to wear a veil on her face and then put pressure on her to learn household work so that she would be *ready* to marry the man who would be her husband: a man whom she had never known or met beforehand. Zubeida finally finds a job as a maid for a French family in Paris.

'In the most traditional rural society, there are no unmarried adolescents. Fifty per cent of the girls are married before reaching puberty, and another thirty-seven per cent in the two years following their puberty.' (Malika Belghiti, *The Relations and the Status of the Rural Family*, Rabat 1970).

The Arab-Islamic Family

THE ROLE OF THE WOMAN in the Arab-Muslim family does not allow for nuances; she is a mother, a sister, or a wife. A woman can never be a friend or a lover. She lives in a society where genders never mix, where she encounters a man only on specific occasions: when she gives birth, has to *report to him* (as a father or a brother) or when she marries him. Only when she produces males does the Arab woman acquire a value in the family or social setting. The rate of divorce of sterile women or mothers of girls is very high in the Arab society. Arab women who are aware of the only weapon they possess, namely their ability to keep their husband and gain the respect of their in-laws by giving birth to boys, often refuse to use contraceptives. The attempts of organizations like family planning associations in Egypt and in South Lebanon have so far failed. These attempts do not take into account the resistance of the Arab women, ready to suffer from a permanent pregnancy rather than to renounce that unique source of 'power' which Arab-Muslim society offers them: the sons, the males, they hope to procreate. 'The Arab countries have the highest birth rate of any region in the world and in the Muslim countries this rate is higher than in the poorest countries of Latin America.' (N. Keddie, *Muslim Women*; Beck, *Women in the Muslim World*, both Harvard University Press).

The relationship between the mother and the male child takes on considerable dimensions in the Arab family and occupies a preponderant place in Muslim society. The mother is the only woman a man can look at, admire and love. The mother recoups all her repressed feelings, the renunciations of her life, through her son, who is her source of pride and survival: she would like to own him forever. The mother of a male child will often interfere to prevent the appearance and growth of love and companionship between her son and her daughter-in-law. She will consistently demand from her son that he takes her side against his wife. In his superb novel *Assarab* (The Mirage), Nagib Mahfuz portrays the relationship between a mother, her son and his wife. A young man from the Cairo petty bourgeoisie marries a young woman who will come to live with him and his mother. The mother is jealous and afraid of losing her power over her son and so prevents any possibility of his having normal sexual relations with his wife, by playing on his respect for his mother. As for him, the only woman who deserves consideration is his mother and any sexual relations with his wife seem incestuous to him. 'Men are only able to love their mother' exclaimed, with bitterness, the Lebanese poetess Ethel Adnan.

Sexuality and Islam

ISLAM HAS ALWAYS been disturbed by woman. In Islam, the woman has never been perceived as a weak human being without a soul or its own will. On the contrary, the Muslim man thinks that women cannot be controlled or tamed and that only real repression of a coercive (not just psychological) nature, even in the legalized form, is required to make them comply to the will of men. The woman is *fitna* in Arabic, meaning beauty and disorder or turmoil. She has a soul which does not carry the weight of an original sin on earth (Islam does not believe that humanity bears a responsibility of original sin). In Islam, sexuality is virtually not condemned as such; it is the woman who must be controlled, as she is a threat to the feeling of security of the man. One should listen to Ibn Qaim al-Iawziya, one of the most orthodox of Muslim theologians, as he described the reasons for pairing: 'Pairing is the most complete gift which has been given to us; it is there that one finds health, pleasure and serenity of the soul'. While Christian piety sets a premium on servile abstinence, in Islam, sexuality must be satisfied so that society may reach a more harmonious condition as a collective, the *umma*. As Islam never believed that the woman preferred to sublimate her sexuality, that she should endure it in order to beget off-spring, Islam decided to confine women's movement to the spaces that the man could control. As the Muslim man and the Muslim woman are sexual beings in a positive sense (the Muslim paradise is a place of eternal sexual enjoyments) the woman will be kept quiet by sharing the man with four other women and concubines, and the man will be able to give vent to his 'promiscuity' in a legal context, with the agreement of the state.

In the words of an Arab saying: 'If a man and a woman gather together the devil is the third person present.' The man will never let his wife stay in a place where other men are present, so she will never be allowed in public places and her right to take care of her own business loses all significance.

Many psychologists and orientalists have looked upon this vision of sexuality and the recognition of a woman *as a feminine being* as constituting a kind of feminism in Islam. The woman exists and has desires in the same way as the man; she has a right to sexual satisfaction in the same way as a man has a right to his pleasure . . . Unfortunately the consequence of that vision leads in the opposite direction than its origin seemed to indicate. As Fatima Mernissi pointed out in *Beyond the Veil*: 'In societies where the seclusion and the surveillance of women is a must, the concept of feminine sexuality is implicitly an active concept.'

Male Arab-Islamic society has protected itself against its own conception of the active sexuality of women by introducing laws which paralyse women's movement and render them totally vulnerable to the desires of men: from the imposition of the veil to the right of the man to repudiate his wife whenever he feels like it, and through to others like the imposition of the male protector or guardian who decides when it is right for a woman to get married or *to go about*.

When an Arab woman walks in the street without a veil or in modern clothes, it does not take long for her to realise that the street is no place for her. When she walks in public places, the men harass her: they feel her as a threat, they feel under attack. The reaction of men is not simply to pay her a compliment or invite her to join them, but on the contrary to throw sexual insults at her, to pursue her for hours. She is perceived as 'an exhibitionist' and must be treated as such. Muslim sexual morality regards women's sexuality as an aggressive element which can threaten the equilibrium of society if it is not controlled. That is why a woman in the street is a symbol of that aggressiveness which manifests itself 'totally freely'.

While Christian morality generally regards the woman's sexuality as passive, Muslim sexual morality sees it quite differently. In the Christian view, there is a tendency to think that the woman endures sexuality as a duty justified by procreation. The Koran and the Muslim tradition do not see things in this way; a balanced Muslim *umma* is a society where sexuality is satisfied. Human beings are not required to reject their sexual instincts but to satisfy them within the limits of the well-being of the Muslim community. And in this context, the woman must be controlled, and her sexuality must be regulated: effectively Islam, which claims to have abolished the promiscuity and the degeneracy which prevailed in the pre-Islamic societies, kept most of the forms of alliance of the *jahiliya* as solely the *man's* privilege. 'Woman's sexuality is what was civilized by Islam.'

Man's sexuality is regarded as promiscuous by Islam and is legalized as such. The man can marry up to four women, since his sexuality is not considered to be exclusive–the man is recognized as unstable and this is why he has the right to divorce whenever he feels like it. In Muslim society it is the woman, and the woman only, who is kept in seclusion and subjugation in order to preserve society's equilibrium, while the man may look for his pleasure where he can find it. 'Women are your fields, go into your fields . . .'.

As long as Islam perceives the sexuality of the woman as an active one, and does not condemn sexuality *as such*, the Islamic state will control the life and activities of its subject through a very harsh control of women's movements and their right to have some independence. 'In societies where the seclusion and the surveillance of women is a must, the concept of feminine sexuality is implicitly an active concept. . . . In Islam it is the woman who is attacked as the personification of destruction and as a symbol of social disorder: she is *fitna* meaning at the same time, both beauty and disorder or turmoil. She is the polarization of what can not be controlled: her sexuality is a lurking danger with a threatening potential'. (Fatima Mernissi, *Beyond the Veil*, Al Saqi Books, London 1985).

IN SUMMARY: if, as soon as a man and a woman are together and alone, they cannot but pair, and if the woman does not reject the sexual act 'naturally' but finds it pleasurable, and if, on top of this, the society where these two people live is a patrilineal one, as is the Muslim society, only one solution is possible: separate the two sexes by confirming the seclusion of the woman. The seclusion of the woman is the result of a relation of forces which works to her disadvantage; it cannot be justified by saying that, given her nature, which is different from man, the woman prefers a life of sacrifice. Such explanations, which justify women's inferior status on the basis of their different nature, were borrowed from western Christianity later on, as the influence of the West grew. This has resulted in chaos and insurmountable contradictions at a conceptual level and in the practice of relations between the two sexes in the Arab World today.

The Arab woman acquires a freedom of movement or the right to move around in male surroundings, to talk with authority with men, only when she reaches an *advanced age*. In other words, when society considers her as a-sexual.

It is because she is not *fitna*, a source of provocation; she is no longer a sexual object with impulses to be kept under control. One often sees a woman over fifty years of age, strengthened by a large male progeniture, smoking, laughing or talking without any difficulty with a group of men. As men say in our culture: 'She is finished' (sexually speaking). It is only then that she can penetrate the world of men, walk in the streets (even in the evenings) without losing the respect of society because of her behaviour.

Salma Botman

WOMEN'S PARTICIPATION IN RADICAL EGYPTIAN POLITICS 1939-1952

THIS ESSAY WILL DISCUSS the role played by women in radical Egyptian politics during the 1940s and early 1950s. The 1940s was a period rich in political ferment, when women's political militancy was made possible by the very structure of state power itself. The state apparatus's weakness and ineffectiveness allowed women to engage in activity in opposition to that of mainstream society. In contrast, when the state's power was consolidated, under the leadership of Gamal Abd al-Nasser from 1952 to 1970, political life was transformed. With bureaucratic centralist philosophy dominant, the militancy of women receded. Indeed, almost all independent activity was quelled.

During the 1940s, small groups of feminists began assessing women's experience in Egypt. In response to the legally and socially based inequality suffered by the mass of Egyptian women, they took action, which meant setting up progressive women's groups and participating in broad-based nationalist and leftist activity. Leftist women, in particular, flourished as artists, political activists and student leaders. Although they were limited in number, their impact was considerable. They demonstrated, at least to those politically active and philosophically liberal, that the problems of Egyptian women were real and demanded serious attention.

Women's participation in the struggles of the Third World are often neglected. This essay, which is based largely on interviews with the activists themselves, is an attempt to acquaint a broad readership with the historic contribution of women in Egypt during a period of radical political upheaval.

The Background

THE PERIOD FROM World War II until the military *coup d'état* of 1952 was a particularly important and dynamic one in Egypt's modern history because of the confluence of two currents: a growing social and political radicalism and a steady deterioration of state control.

The 1940s and early 1950s were years of relative political freedom characterized by a rising militancy among those dissatisfied with the political hierarchy's inability to win full independence from the British and among those committed to shaping Egypt into a strong and prosperous country. This was also a time when the intermittent weakness of state authority was the most significant fact of Egyptian political life. The state's lack of cohesion and the ineffectiveness of the political police allowed a dynamic nationalist spirit to prevail: new political organizations and philosophies were expressed and dissenting ideas were publicized through a vibrant oppositional press.

Although, according to the 1923 Constitution, Egypt had the forms of a semi-liberal society, that is the forms of Western democracy, it lacked its content. Freedom of speech, of association and of the press were fragile rights granted or rescinded depending on the strength and unity of the government itself. Political life was marked by an enfeebled and inexperienced party system represented by statesmen, some of whom had little commitment to the democratic process.

Instability in the political arena prevented parliamentary democracy from firmly taking root and from spreading beyond a narrow sector of political life. With the exception of the Wafd Party, which saw itself and was seen by others as the image of liberal democracy in Egypt and which at different times could count on the support of the entire nation, mainstream political parties in Egypt were little more than the expression of the personalities who monopolized and manipulated them. For the most part, they neglected social and economic reform, subjugating them to the lowest common denominator of Egyptian political life: the demand for independence.

With few exceptions, political work was performed by Egyptian men who, through family prominence, wealth, political connections or the patronage system, rose up the legislative ladder. Women participated in public affairs only sporadically, essentially because Egyptian society was socially traditional and highly conservative. Men and women were generally separated, both in the private domain of the house and in the more public sphere of the street. The family was the nucleus of society and most decisions were expected to derive from it. Marriages were still arranged and women were regarded as the legitimate object of men's possession. Having limited input into or experience with the higher levels of government, education, business or professional life, women on the whole did not exert a powerful force in national affairs.

The inequality suffered by women was both legally and socially based. While Islamic law allowed a woman to own property, carry out business and inherit a portion of her father's estate equal to half her brother's share, it put her at her husband's mercy in matters concerning divorce and the family. Even in their private lives, most women were not always afforded the same respect due any man; the majority of women were dependent and obedient, but there were exceptions.

Among intellectuals of the haute and petite bourgeoisie, the traditional ways of thinking existed with less force. Within the more cosmopolitan world of leftist politics or in the French *lycée* and the university, men and women were mingling together socially and academically, barriers were breaking down and conventional roles were being challenged. While young, modern emancipated Egyptian women were a minority in the 1940s, they did exist and some went on to become leaders of the leftist, women's, and student movements. So while Egyptian women suffered their measure of oppression, they were not merely victims of male manipulation. Albeit in an unrecognized way, women have contributed to Egypt's modern development – despite the country's severe social backwardness and the traditional values which many ascribe to the Islamic religion.

Women's participation in grassroots Egyptian politics dates back at least to the 1919 revolution, when Egyptian women protested against the British occupation and demonstrated in the streets alongside male members of their families. A few women were even jailed for short periods of time in consequence of their political activity. Groups of 'gentlewomen' began a social revolution when they threw off their veils, rejected the harem and began organizing Egypt's social services. After World War I, a movement to emancipate women was organized and led by women from some of Egypt's most prominent families. They argued that the improvement of women's condition would contribute to the general welfare and must not be ignored. Women also belonged to the nationalist Wafd Party, participated in the anti-fascist groups which proliferated in Egypt during the 1930s, and in the 1940s joined the budding underground Communist movement.

Inge Aflatun, a well-known political activist, feminist and gifted artist described her background and introduction to politics:

'I was born in Cairo into a family of large landowners. Education was important and many of my family studied abroad. . . . The family spoke French which was typical of bourgeois families at that time. . . . My introduction to politics came through the social and economic conditions of the time. I was shocked by the poverty and by the differences between classes. I felt this by instinct. I began painting when I was young but I was not happy about it. . . . Then came an important event . . . in 1941 while I was still a student at the French *lycée*. A Trotskyite artist who was also very poor . . . gave me art lessons for two or three years. He opened the world to me by asking, "What is art? What is life?" . . . My art exploded at that time; I had now found painting. . . . I also began questioning and searching for solutions to questions that were raised in my studies and in my life. The dissatisfaction I felt was present in my first paintings. Even the critics commented on this, saying that the artist was in a state of revolt; some hinted that it was sexual frustration. At the *lycée*, I met people, discussed things, found Marxist books, was in contact with young Egyptian intellectuals. Then I became a Marxist. . . . My entrance into politics and my painting were two ways to search for my country. My Arabic language skills were not very good, so at the age of seventeen I began to learn Arabic.'

Latifa al-Zayat, a student leader in the university in 1946, later to become a writer and novelist, recollected:

'I was born in 1924, in a small down, Damietta, overlooking the Mediterranean . . . into a lower middle class or upper petty bourgeois family . . . and I came to Cairo in 1936 for my education. I began university in 1942-43 . . . By the time I was in university, I lost all hope in the existing parties because they failed to answer the national question. I became a Marxist or a Communist from a nationalist point of view. What appealed to me very much in Marxism . . . was the ethics . . . the absence of discrimination in religion, race, sex. . . . I was tired of the hypocrisy, cowardice, caution and trembling of the class I belonged to.'

It was World War II and its consequences that prompted leftist and feminist-minded women to become increasingly interested in and articulate about the problems affecting women in Egypt; particularly those which reflected prejudicial treatment in jobs, salaries, education and family life. Not only did the war stimulate industry and hasten the proletarianization of the masses, it also deeply involved Egypt in international politics and gave evidence of the continued dominance of the British in the Nile Valley. With shortages in food and the population increasing faster than the development of land or industry, the condition of the vast majority of the populace was worsening. The war aggravated social problems and made the reality of inequality even more jarring. The radicalism born at this time emerged directly out of the essence of war and dislocation.

Swelling the ranks of the dissatisfied were sections of the petty bourgeoisie, radical students, workers and women. Organizationally, the beneficiaries of this discontent were the Communists, the Muslim fundamentalists, democrats and radical nationalists. While they were separately participating in anti-British activity, giving new energy to the nationalist movement, by the war's end their complaints had become clearer. They opposed the staggering inflation, chronic shortages, increasing joblessness and massive social, legal and economic inequities. Moreover, they grew more combative as traditional political forces in Egypt were weakening and the policies they supported were being denounced. The King was discredited, the most important mainstream nationalist party, the Wafd, was divided by right-wing factionalism, other rival political parties were engaged in personality conflicts, and negotiations with the British for independence seemed doomed to failure. There was movement amongst workers in the form of labour disputes and strikes. There was a growing feminist response to gender-based inequalities. It was in this environment, then, that the illegal communist movement and the open feminist activity which it spawned developed and operated.

Women and the Communist Movement

THERE ARE TWO stages of Egyptian communist activity in the twentieth century. The first occurred in the early 1920s, when the Egyptian Socialist/Communist Party was created. The Party, with an almost exclusively male membership, played a radicalizing role in the nascent trade union movement, but because it refused to participate in broad-based nationalist activity to challenge the British occupation, it became isolated from the main currents of political activity. After a few years the Party was driven underground and then ultimately disappeared, leaving a vacuum in Egyptian Marxism from the mid-1920s until the late 1930s.

The communist movement revived during the early years of World War II. Despite the commitment and energy of its membership, it suffered from a number of weaknesses. First, there was no unified Communist Party in the 1940s. The movement was made up of separate, rival organizations. Diversity led to fragmentation and internecine hostility, which weakened the impact of Marxism in the country. Second, there was a noticeable dissociation between the communists and the Egyptian masses, which was most obviously reflected in the composition of the communist movement – middle class and, at least at the beginning of this period, led by one of Egypt's ethnic minorities – Jewish Egyptians. In essence, the movement was small in numbers, urban and highly intellectual, recruiting mainly students and professionals. Some skilled workers active in trade union affairs were organized, but they were decidedly in the minority. The village was virtually ignored, given the wide class and cultural gaps that separated the members of the communist movement from the mass of poor peasants.

Despite its structural and organizational limitations and its inexperience, however, the Marxist movement was capable of exerting sporadic influence on the nationalist, labour, feminist and student scenes. Moreover, communism had a significant ideological impact on Egyptian society and was able to help undermine Egypt's ineffectual political system and create an atmosphere in which radical nationalist military officers could operate and ultimately overthrow Egypt's royalist regime. Communists helped break down the country's exclusive social hierarchy through demonstrations, organization and the publication of oppositional newspapers and pamphlets. In fact, in an important way, the communists contributed to the tradition of dissident thought which has since become a significant part of Egypt's political, intellectual and artistic life.

The Egyptian communist movement of the 1940s and early 1950s was largely male – but the women who were involved in the movement were equally dedicated and hard working in their commitments. Sharing, for the most part, a common world-view, these young militants created a society of their own in which they made friends and chose spouses, in which they learned lessons and taught their experiences. In this context, plans – and dreams – for the future were developed.

Women were recruited into the communist movement, educated and given assignments on the basis of their commitment, not as a function of their gender. They were involved in committee work and in demonstrations, in leafleting outside factories and in agitating on university campuses. But the specific problems of women neither dominated communist activity nor captivated the leftist mind. Essentially, the Left focused its attention on ending the British occupation of Egypt and it concentrated its resources on recruiting, besides already enlightened intellectuals, radical trade unionists who were overwhelmingly male.

The women who were organized in underground groups were self-sacrificing in the extreme. Involvement in illegal activity meant that every aspect of their lives was affected: family ties, work, friendships, and aspirations. A commitment to the Party implied promises of time, discipline, obedience, hard work and family disapproval. It also suggested a dual role for women – as general political activists and as feminists. While they grappled with the twin issues of national independence and women's liberation, within the communist movement, almost alone, women championed the social, legal, political and economic rights of women. Although communist men theoretically supported female liberation, they believed and convinced the women themselves to accept that the primary struggle of Egyptian Marxism was against the British occupation of the country. Leftist women, then, directed most of their efforts toward the general political front where they thought the greatest progress could be achieved. Also, because of the severe underdevelopment in Egypt, with the bulk of women lagging far behind men politically and educationally, it was extremely difficult to build an effective national democratic women's organization. Latifa al-Zayat noted:

'It is a luxury to think of the liberation of women . . . when you see your brothers, fathers and children strangled, scorned and exploited by foreigners and local men and women. It is only when civilization reaches a certain level, that the problems of women, children and minorities become urgent. Women make the most noble contribution to the liberation of society when they embrace causes outside themselves and outside their families. . . . One of the basic teachings of Marxism is that the individual cannot be free or liberated without his society being free and liberated. Women's fight for liberation implies a fight for the liberation of society.'

Women participated at every level of the communist movement, from the highest level of the central committee down to the cell. This did not mean that every or even most communist men accepted the notion of equality with women. Indeed, within the leftist movement itself, women made efforts to combat reactionary ideology by circulating materials concerning women's role in the socialist cause and in society at large and by writing, in internal party newspapers, about exclusively female issues and problems.

In the main, the communist women were of bourgeois and petty-bourgeois origin. There were daughers of large landlords and there were even the children of a few distinguished pashas but the majority were inescapably middle class. Their fathers may have been involved in business, the liberal professions, agricultural enterprise; they may have been employed by the public or private sector in 'white collar' positions.

Communist women had roots in Upper Egypt and the Delta, in Cairo and Alexandria. Although they originally came from towns and villages as well as the larger cities, for the most part, their involvement in underground activity dated from their arrival in Cairo or Alexandria to work or to study. Recruitment into the communist movement took place in the French *lycée*, in the university and at political clubs such as The House of Scientific Research, which was the legal front group for a clandestine Marxist organization. The House of Scientific Research, which served as an important 'theoretical school' for cadres, included a women's committee which comprised between thirty and fifty women. Discussions about feminism, the national movement, fascism, imperialism and the social situation in European countries were not uncommon.

Most women were attracted to the Marxist movement when they were under twenty-five years old. They were young and idealist and they had the leisure to think, question and discuss the issues of the day. What the Left offered women was an alternative to the mainstream political parties which many believed had failed Egypt. Marxist ideas represented a fundamental critique of the structure of Egyptian society and Marxism posed answers to questions of underdevelopment and political conservatism.

Women were often promoted and arrested in the same ways as their male colleagues, but not with the same frequency. Given the traditional nature of Egyptian society, where women were primarily wives and mothers, the Left considered it adventurous to place women in the forefront of communist activity. Still, the women who engaged in militant feminist activity camouflaged their communist ties for fear of official repression. Soraya Adham, active in the 1940s, recalled one of her experiences as a professional revolutionary:

'I left my house [in 1948] and had to live all by myself, which was difficult for a woman to do at this time. I remember once I was living in a furnished room in the Bulaq section of Cairo. One night the whole of Bulaq district was saturated by police who were looking for Marxists and Muslim fundamentalists. I was new in the house. It was two o'clock in the morning and I heard the landlady knocking on my door asking if the police could be let in to have a look. I told them one moment while I dress; when I opened the door, they saw a woman living alone. They asked me my name and why I wasn't living with my family. I gave them my name and explained that I had had a quarrel with my family. The police officer said: "Tomorrow I will come and take you home and make peace with your family because a girl of a good family should not live alone." I agreed. And in the morning I told the landlady that I was going back to my family and I left the house. When the police officer told the political police my name, his superior said: "She is the one we are searching for." When they came back to the house, I, of course, had left.'

Later, when she was found, she spent two months in prison; the following year she was jailed for ten months. Many of her feminist comrades were similarly apprehended and served their share of sentences as political prisoners.

Women were not mistreated in prison, but they could not expect any dispensations as a result of their sex. According to the communist newspaper *al-Malayin* (*The Millions*), the prison administration isolated political prisoners from the rest of the inmate population (which was against regulations), forbade all books and reading and writing materials, interrogated and hand searched the prisoners, forced some to wear prison clothing, provided the poorest food (consisting of lentils and *ful* beans with liquorice) and prohibited visits from families.

In sum, while there was at least formal interest in the women's movement among progressive men, in practice women received little more than organizational sympathy from the communist groups; there was very little structural cooperation. As a result, Marxist women took their ideas outside the leftist movement. Their intention was to raise the level of political consciousness of other progressive women who were not necessarily organized in political associations.

Radical Feminist Activity

WHEN PROGRESSIVE women began thinking about how they might effect improvements in the status of women in society, they concluded that broad-based and legal activity would offer the greatest results. Moreover, they recognized that membership in the communist movement would not necessarily guarantee successful work among women. The activity they planned was bifurcated in design, with the intention of reaching both domestic and international audiences. Within Egypt, leftist women formed small feminist societies essentially limited to women in higher institutes and universities – women who were most naturally predisposed to radical feminist ideas of change. Women also joined the staffs of newspapers and wrote columns devoted to the concerns of women, they participated in legal political and nationalist work in the academy and they made efforts to popularize such strictly female issues as equality in the workplace, improved day care facilities and greater female participation in the political process. Internationally, through delegations of Egyptian women travelling abroad to conferences, the world community was familiarized with Egyptian social and political problems.

In Egypt, progressive women did not work through existing women's organizations largely because of ideological differences which were too serious to bridge: while radical women advocated the social transformation of Egyptian society, mainstream feminists supported more limited emancipation. As a result, the Marxists set up new groups and The League of Women Students and Graduates from the University and Egyptian Institutes was created in 1944/45. The League included some fifty women and, although built on the achievements of earlier feminists, was the first women's organization in Egypt that adopted radical views about women and women's role in revolutionary society.

The group was set up to identify and defend women's interests. From the beginning, its radical, anti-imperialist complexion was apparent. A pamphlet published by the organization announced:

' . . . Struggle for the widest freedoms, struggle for liberation from oppression, hunger and aggression; struggle by ourselves and for ourselves; . . . struggle to create a free, noble life for Egyptian women under the sovereignty of a free and noble country; struggle to realize democratic freedom for women in Egypt – that is the freedom which cannot arrive under the shadow of the imperialist and imperialism nor under the shadow of enslavement and exploitation.'

In a society as traditional and socially conservative as Egypt, these were exceptionally radical ideas. Since the vast number of Egyptian women, and men, either did not have the opportunity to think about such change or simply were not prepared to accept it, the League was restricted in membership and discreet about its activities.

Certainly, the ideas of women's emancipation had earlier roots in Egypt, but in the mid-1940s they began to take on more concrete and controversial dimensions. The issues embraced by the League spanned the social, economic and political realms: the right of all women to vote; the responsibility of the state to set up children's nurseries and guarantee social insurance and security; equal pay for equal work; the inauguration of democracy.

The League neither constituted itself as a political party nor aspired to become one. Although a number of the League's members were already active communists, the group did not have as its goal the recruitment of women into the underground movement. Instead, it conceived of itself essentially as a gathering place for young women who were interested in both the narrowly gender oriented problems of women and the larger difficulties challenging Egypt as a nation – in particular, the struggle against British colonialism.

The League, however, was never able to develop its potential, having lived only a short life; it was closed down by the Prime Minister in July 1946 when, from a temporary position of strength, the government struck down its political opposition. In total, twelve 'hostile' groups were brought to an end. It is interesting that the authorities thought that the women's organization was threatening enough to warrant closure.

During the existence of the League, the first World Congress of Women, organized by the Fédération Démocratique Internationale des Femmes was held in Paris in November of 1945. A number of Egyptian communist women were sent to the Conference. The two main themes of the meeting were the condemnation of fascism and imperialism and the end of inequality between men and women. Inge Aflatun described her experience in Paris:

'I was chosen to lead the Egyptian delegation. I was very excited; I saw many brave and famous women. The Soviet delegation, I remember, came in their military uniforms with their medals shining; they had just come from the war. All of what we saw there left a great impression. I made a very powerful speech in which I linked the oppression of women in Egypt to the British occupation and imperialism. I not only denounced the British, but the King and the politicians as well. It was a very political speech in which I called for national liberation and the liberation of women. My ideas were applauded.'

Immediately upon their return to Cairo, Inge Aflatun and several other communist women were detained by the police, held and questioned for three hours. The police, having somehow learned of the radical views expressed in Paris, apprehended the three as a demonstration of the authorities' severe disapproval of their behaviour. Taken into custody to frighten and perhaps intimidate them, they were later released as a result of insufficient criminal evidence against them. In reaction to the treatment she received, Inge Aflatun later brought a lawsuit against the political police accusing it of misconduct. In consequence, she was the subject of continuous harassment by the police for years to come.

After the war, there was a continuous female presence in the student and nationalist movements. In the 1946 nationalist demonstrations which momentarily unhinged the Egyptian authorities, women not only participated, but some became leaders. It was said that when the communist Latifa al-Zayat, for example, addressed a university audience, she set the students on fire with her dynamism and zeal. Al-Zayat was then elected to a university-wide student committee. She recalled:

'I stood for election, and not a man, because I had more chance of success than he. I had an appeal, an ability to deal with students, to talk to them, persuade and win them over. . . . I as a woman was accepted by the mass of students as a student secretary, at a time when the percentage of women at the university was only about 5 per cent.'

But there was not complete acceptance of women's participation in university politics. Al-Zayat continued:

' . . . I fought against the Muslim fundamentalist groups which tried to defame my reputation – they called me a prostitute and other such things. I remember I went home and wept. But I said: "This is public work, this is not the last time I will be defamed." This turned me into a puritan. Really, because they said that . . . communists were immoral . . . communists became puritans, to maintain their image with the public, especially those who were working in close connection with the masses.'

Confirming the harassment to which politically active women were subjected by more traditional forces, another militant, Soraya Adham added:

' . . . Everyone of the [leftist] girls used to walk circled by our male comrades and friends so that the Muslim fundamentalists would not obstruct us. . . . In 1948, I was beaten by some of them for participating in political activity.'

Provocation did not deter women from continuing their political activity. When the Peace Movement was established in 1950 in Egypt, it attracted women and included among its leaders Inge Aflatun. Also, the Women's Committee for Popular Resistance was formed in October 1951, to support the nationalist fighting which had broken out in the

Suez Canal Zone: it was endorsed, in the main, by progressive women. The aim of the group was to help the resistance against the British occupation both materially and morally. Although women could not fight, they could visit the area and report on the conditions they found. Inge Aflatun stated:

'A women's delegation secretly went to the Zone for a day. There were two zones then–one for the British occupation forces and one for the people. We told the British that we were going to visit the wounded in hospital to give presents. In fact, without knowing anyone in advance, we went to the popular quarter, met some workers in the street and told them our ideas about forming this resistance group. They brought us to many women's houses and we talked. When we returned to Cairo we held a press conference. . . . People did not know that the men had poor clothing, too few jackets. We publicized the situation and our activity was successful.'

In the press conference they held, the women's delegation publicized the difficult conditions of the *fidayin*, the freedom fighters, denounced colonialism and demanded that the principles of the United Nations Charter respecting national sovereignty be enacted. The Committee was successful in focusing increased national attention on the Suez Canal not only in 1951 but also in 1956, in protest against the tripartite (British, French, Israeli) aggression against Egypt of that year.

The projects initiated by women in the 1940s and 1950s were short-lived partly because of the lack of mass support but also due to the occasional pressure of governmental interference. Still, women did have some success in bringing the feminist issue to the attention of the politically conscious through political agitation, organization and journalism. They demonstrated, at least to other intellectuals, that the problems of Egyptian women were real and deserved serious attention. To raise the women's issue to the realm of a respectable political cause was their intention–all the while embracing wider political questions and especially that of the national liberation of Egypt.

Conclusion

ALTHOUGH IT MAY BE SAID that Egyptian women in the 1940s were on the margins of political activity, they were not 'hidden from history'. In fact, women were active and creative during this time and what made their militancy possible at all was the very structure of state power itself.

The state's vulnerability and periodic ineffectiveness allowed women to engage in political activity and to popularize views in opposition to those of mainstream society. In essence, when governmental weakness prevailed in Egypt, diversity was tolerated and even encouraged. But when the state's authority was consolidated and reinforced, political and artistic life was transformed. From the early 1950s onward, and especially during the rule of Gamal Abd al-Nasser (1952-70), bureaucratic centralist philosophy dominated. With this, the state became stronger and the militancy of women receded. Indeed, almost all independent political action was quelled and the heterogeneity so attractive in the 1940s disappeared. Communism, and the important feminist voice within it, was subdued and even at times coopted. Under Nasser, the communist movement became further divided between those who upheld Nasser's efforts as progressive and those who could not reconcile these measures with his overtly anti-democratic and punitive ones. Likewise, the independent feminist activity so inspirational in the decade before Nasser's coup came to a sudden end with the arrival of the military government. It is only within the last few years that the Egyptian feminist movement has been revived. Still in embryonic form, it faces the difficult problem of how to organize and attract adherents in a country where the mass of the population lives on the margins of subsistence.

Hamida Kazi

PALESTINIAN WOMEN AND THE NATIONAL LIBERATION MOVEMENT : A SOCIAL PERSPECTIVE

WOMEN HAVE ALWAYS PARTICIPATED in struggles for national liberation, and a few of them are glorified for what they do. However, the essence of their role in political struggles has always been ignored, just as it is ignored in economic development. This leaves the social sphere, where women's subordination is a generally accepted phenomenon. It is within this socially subordinate position that the non-recognition of women's participation or rather, the lack of participation in national liberation movements needs to be analysed. There are three important dimensions to this analysis: (i) The role of women assumes secondary significance because of the nature of the task they perform; (ii) Women's participation in, and their position in, the national struggle is regulated by the class structure of the movement; (iii) Women do not participate in the movement en masse – not because of their lack of politicization, but on account of social constraints. Besides, if and when women are incorporated in the struggle as the necessity arises, as in the case of Algerian women, then rather than participating, women are used. However, Palestinian women have a long history of creating women's organizations and of participating in the struggle for the security and liberation of their

*Although the paper is written with a view on Palestinian women's participation in general in the national struggle, it mostly focuses on women on the West Bank.

homeland. Today, when the Palestinian cause has eventually received world recognition, it is worth analysing the contemporary struggle of Palestinian women in a historical context. Alongside this, we shall also examine the three dimensions of analysis cited above.

A Brief History of the Struggle of Palestinian Women

WOMEN'S PARTICIPATION in the struggle of the Palestinians for their homeland can be divided into three stages. The first stage dates from the beginning of the establishment of the Zionist settlements in 1882 to the creation of the state of Israel in 1948. The second stage extends from 1948 to June 1967 – the end of the June war and the beginning of the Israeli occupation of the West Bank and Gaza. The third stage is the contemporary on-going struggle.

These divisions provide a convenient framework for understanding the historical development of women's struggle. It is important here to note that since 1948 the Palestinian struggle has had to face repeated disruption and displacement and has been waged from the disapora as well as in the Occupied Territories. In both places there are obstacles, but the struggle is a single and unified one.

(i) In the first stage, the participation of women was passive, inarticulate and unorganized. Under a strict social order, freedom of movement for women was almost non-existent. However, in 1884 women for the first time participated alongside men in raising their voices against the first Jewish settlement (near the town of 'Afulah). In November 1917, after the end of the First World War, they took part in huge demonstrations at the time of the Balfour Declaration.[1] In 1921, Palestinian women took their first step towards organized activities by setting up a society – The Arab Women's Society, based in Jerusalem. It played an important role in organizing demonstrations against Zionist settlements. It ceased to exist after only two years, due to the lack of funding and the social and political pressure which was put on women. Shortly afterwards, however, women formed a 'rescue committee' to collect donations, and they revived it. During the 1929 rebellion, women took part in protests and demonstrations and a number of women were killed by British forces. They also organized a Women's Conference. The conference sent a protest letter to the King of England and to the League of Nations (now the UN). They also formed a 14-member delegation to meet the High Commissioner demanding that the Balfour Declaration be revoked and Jewish immigration halted.

During the 1936 rebellion, women began to collect funds and distribute them among people in need, especially the families of the detainees. They delivered weapons, food and water to the men in the struggle. In 1948, when Israeli forces had already covered most parts of Palestine and fighting broke out in the streets, one woman (Helwa Zaidan) is known to have picked up her son's weapons after he and his father were killed before her eyes, and to have fought until she too was killed. On 10 April 1948, at the Deir Yassin massacre, a school teacher lost her life while giving first aid to the injured Palestinians.

(ii) The second stage, from 1948 to 1967, is characterized by a retreat from direct struggle. During this time social, charitable and superficial political activities are dominant. Women's participation was usually shaped by the ideology of the male leadership, which could not take direct action, either in occupied Palestine, now Israel, or in the West Bank that became part of Jordan. Women made some headway in economic activity and education. Within Israel's 1948 border, Palestinian social, political and educational institutions were under the threat of closure and all the restrictions imposed by the newly established state of Israel had in fact gravely limited the chances of continuing the struggle. Resistance activities remained confined to a small group of educated women mainly from the bourgeois class. In the West Bank, most Palestinians became absorbed in the Jordanian system. For the educated Palestinians, their professions, education and everything else were linked with Jordan. Thus resistance meant the loss of everything and poor Palestinians in the refugee camps had even fewer options open to them. However, after the establishment of the Palestine Liberation Organization in 1964, the Palestinian Women's Association was set up, through which women took part in the first session of the Palestinian National Council held in Jerusalem. By now economic survival had become a major issue for most Palestinians. Loss of land for agrarian people, especially immediately after 1948, meant the agrarian population entering into wage labour and a new process of proletarianization of the Palestinian peasantry began, which women too could not escape. Despite religious values and strict social control it was essential for families to allow women to enter into waged employment. This certainly provided women with freedom of movement (although we must emphasize that freedom of movement does not necessarily lead to other kinds of freedom such as freedom in decision-making). In these circumstances, education became the most significant element of Palestinian society (Palestinians have the highest rate of literacy in the Arab world).

In 1965, the Palestinian Women's Association held its first conference, and later it was to set up branches in different parts of the West Bank. The association was banned by the Jordanian regime in 1966. However, in the late 1960s women became very active – although women's groups consisted of mainly educated middle-class women.

(iii) The third stage of women's struggle in the Palestinian liberation movement can be divided into two parts: from June 1967 until 1970, and from then onwards.

From 1967 to 1972, armed struggle was a dominant aspect of the Palestinian movement. The role of women was not confined to delivering food and weapons to the *fidayin* (Palestinian freedom fighters). They also took part in the planning and carrying out of armed operations. Laila Khalid is perhaps the best known among them. Many women were sent to prison for anti-occupation activities. In the West Bank and Gaza, women were active in demonstrations, public meetings and so on. However, there is little they can do under conditions of occupation. Since 1967, the Israeli occupation has created enormous constraints on all kinds of activities; for anything from armed struggle to collecting herbs (*za'tar*) in the mountains people may be subjected to military detention.

From 1967 to 1982, women were freely mobilized. In fact during this period women began to wrestle with the not unique dilemma of reconciling participation in the national struggle and their reproductive role while the continued existence of three and a half million Palestinians dispersed all over the world is under threat, as is the survival of Palestinian culture.

Women under colonialism face the dilemma of a double struggle – against foreign domination and against societal oppression. However, for Palestinian women this dilemma has additional problems. The most crucial of these is that one part of Palestine has become Israel, and the rest is occupied by Israel. Nearly three and a half million Palestinians are dispersed all over the world. It is hard to get an exact breakdown of their numbers in the various countries of the diaspora. However, the following table is based on PLO, Israeli and UN statistics. According to the UN, 641,000 of these live in 59 refugee camps in Lebanon, Syria, Jordan, the West Bank and Gaza (because of the 1982 Israeli attack on Lebanon and its consequences, the Palestinian population there has dropped considerably). Also, while colonialism in other countries has been a political force, in Palestine there is an added religious aspect which makes the

Table 1. Palestinian Population

Country	Population
Israel (1967 borders)	520,000
West Bank and Gaza	1,100,000
Jordan	960,000
Lebanon	260,000
Syria	170,000
Egypt	35,000
Kuwait	170,000
Libya	7,000
Saudi Arabia	25,000
Iraq	15,000
United Arab Emirate	18,000
The US, Latin America and Europe	165,000
Total	3,445,000

colonizers even more determined to keep control.[2] Furthermore, continuous dispersion of the population since 1948 has had a destructive effect on the community life of the Palestinian people.[3] Finally, due to the fact that there is no home base for the struggle, the national liberation movement is displaced every time a host country decides to close its doors on the Palestinian people (always of course in its own national interest!) In view of these circumstances, the movement has also to fight for its own continuity. These factors create an even more difficult position for Palestinian women, and reinforce traditional oppression, this time through political necessity. On the one hand it is not participation in the national struggle but the struggle itself that faces annihilation, and on the other, in the absence of any state or government of their own, the family assumes a strong institutional character and women find themselves as the bearers of Palestinian culture which only they can keep alive wherever they may be.

It should be emphasized that this predicament makes it all the more imperative for Palestinian women to involve themselves in the Liberation Movement. The leadership of the Palestinian Liberation Movement seem to have recognized the seriousness of this fact, especially after the 1967 war. However, to what extent it has been innovative in regard to the role, we shall attempt to analyse in the discussion that follows.

Women's mobilization in the contemporary national struggle

AS WE MENTIONED EARLIER, the present phase of Palestinian women's struggle dates from 1967. At this time it became the movement's policy to recruit women. The defeat of the Arab forces in 1967 once again strengthened the idea in the Palestinian mind that women's participation was essential for the success of their struggle. Women had always contributed to the national cause in all struggles. They became visibly involved in the movement and were given military training. Mostly, however, their work was channeled into support activities such as nursing, the provision of food and uniforms for the fighters and also the setting up and developing of social and cultural institutions, which were an extension of women's 'natural' skills. Thus, 'female participation in the PLO structure verges on little more than tokenism,' (Haddad, 1980; 162).

The situation changed after 1970, especially in Jordan but also in the rest of the diaspora as women began to participate in the armed struggle. However, the extent of women's involvement in this regard depended not only on themselves, but to a greater degree on the support they received from their families, particularly the men in the family. Thus, although women were sent out on missions alongside men, their participation remained sporadic. To argue that women lacked the opportunity to become actively involved in the armed struggle does not in any way undermine their support activities. But the categorization of activities in this way separates the women's world from that of men, where all non-domestic activities are dominant. It simply extends the public/private dichotomy to the mass movement in which men and women are segregated according to a socially conventional division of labour.

It may be argued, though, that Palestinian women themselves have been aware of the under-utilization of their participative abilities and that the national liberation movement basically lacked a theory of armed struggle relating to social change (Sayigh, 1985). Thus social reality was not conducive to women's active participation in the movement. In addition, a large number of women remained deprived of their role in the struggle. This critique did not go unnoticed by the movement. For example, provisions were made for women to obtain technical and professional skills. These provisions were made for camp women in particular. In addition, much attention was given to literacy among women, and income-generating projects helped those in need to become self-sufficient. Unfortunately, the Israeli invasion of 1982 brought about yet another disruption, with serious consequences for women's contribution to the movement.

Women in the West Bank

The role of women in the West Bank requires further analysis. It must be noted that under occupation the very existence of every Palestinian is thereatened. Economically the society is in ruins; politically, the occupying authority has one aim – to crush any sign of Palestinian activism. After nineteen years of occupation, it became increasingly difficult to carry on the struggle in the face of measures such as collective punishment and the demolition of houses of those even suspected of being involved in the struggle. According to a 1984 UN report, between 1967 and 1982 1,346 houses were demolished and new measures included the sealing of house or rooms with concrete. Other obstructions such as the closure of academic institutions and house arrests are ongoing phenomena. Another common tactic is deportation; this deprives the Palestinians not only of their home and family, but also of their ability to carry on the struggle.

This is only the tip of the iceberg. The psychological effects of the occupation, particularly on women, are beyond description. Despite all the restrictions and problems, the struggle for liberation continues, albeit with frequent interruptions. Women's participation under these conditions is extremely difficult and the social system itself represents further obstacles since in Muslim culture the place of woman is separated from that of men. However, occupation has also produced some underlying contradictory forces which have led to women's participation in many areas of life. For example, despite social inhibitions, the rate of female employment has increased since the 1967 war from 8.4 per cent in 1968 to 24.8 per cent in 1980 (UN report, 1984). Here, though, it must be emphasized that this increase in female employment has not occurred as a result of a thriving economy. On the contrary, the West Bank has no independent economy of its own and there is no Palestinian financial or banking system. Whatever economy existed under Jordanian control before the occupation when the West Bank was part of Jordan is now controlled by and channeled through Israel.

The result of this is that the Occupied Territories have been witnessing a decline in agricultural and economic development. In addition, the continuous expropriation of Palestinian land and the seizure of control over water resources by the Israeli authorities has resulted in a number of changes in the labour market, including the economic status of women and their patterns of employment. Besides repressive economic conditions, political oppression such as deportation, imprisonment and the migration of male members of the family have obliged many women to take up employment. Thus a woman's income is vital for the survival of the family. A great number of women go to work in Israel as migrant agricultural workers. Palestinian women's labour is also being exploited by Israeli enterprises set up in the Occupied Territories. These enterprises specialise in finishing goods such as garments imported from Israel and the wages women receive are nearly 50 per cent lower than wages for equivalent work in Israel. Awareness of such exploitative practices and their vulnerable economic-political situation has strengthened women's determination to fight against occupation. Despite the odds, women have been contributing to the struggle for liberation. The Popular Front for the Liberation of Palestine (PFLP) and of course other groups have been active in organizing women. Initially activities included political disobedience, the distribution of pamphlets and even smuggling arms. However, women's participation in the resistance remained confined to young and educated middle-class women.[4] Women have also been active in women's work committees but these have mostly been concerned with the educational and social welfare of ordinary women.

For their participation in political activities, such as demonstrations against occupation, writing for newspapers and other forms of opposition to the occupation, women have been imprisoned. It is not unusual even for girls attending university or high-school to be sentenced to short-term or in some cases long-term detention. Education is another field in which women's participation is increasing, since it is considered a significant aspect of their resistance against occupation. Thus, in the 1981/82 session female students constituted 40 per cent of the total number of students in institutions of higher education on the West Bank. However, one should not conclude from these figures that the position of women in Palestinian society has altered considerably or that their participation in the national struggle is greater than in other movements. The consequences of the education and employment of women can of course be seen in their social and political consciousness. As women and men in Palestinian society have switched from farming to waged labour, the proletarianization of women has led to women's entry into trade unions, where they are very active.

A critique of women's activities in the national liberation movement

WE MENTIONED EARLIER that Palestinian women's organizations date back as far as 1921. Today there are about 38 officially registered women's charitable organizations on the West Bank alone.[5] The broad spectrum of social activities undertaken by these organizations include child-care and health and literacy programmes, and the creation of self-reliance and vocational training centres and income-generating projects. In addition, the growing realization of the significance of women's participation in the national struggle led to the formation of four women's committees in the late 1970s and early 1980s. The first of these was the Women's Work Committee set up in Ramallah in 1978 by a group of highly educated and ideologically and politically motivated women. It aimed to reaching large numbers of women and to mobilize them to join the women's and national movements. It developed rapidly in many parts of the Occupied Territories, reaching a membership in the range of two thousand. However, growth also brought problems; there were debates on priorities and the emphasis given to different issues. A Working Women's Committee was then formed whose priority was to make working women aware of their threefold oppression – that originating in the traditional patriarchal nature of society; that to be found at the workplace; and that caused by Israeli occupation. Through their struggle at the workplace, in many organizations they have won a paid holiday on 8 March, International Women's Day.[6]

In 1982, two other committees, the Palestine Women's Committee and the Women's Committee for Social Work, were formed in the same way. While women in all these committees are active in the unionization of working women, generating social and political consciousness, supporting prisoners' families etc, the divisions which led to the establishment of the four different committees seem to reflect the factionalist trend in the larger movement (Al-Helous, Lends, 1986). The membership of these committees reflect the ideological views of the factions in the larger movements itself. Moreover, as the women's groups are part of the national liberation movement, their programmes and policies are linked to the movement's wider policies, which it might be argued are in the interest of Palestinian people in general.

However, the policies are conspicuous for their segregation of the world of women from that of men. Although there are women in the forefront of the armed struggle – for example Fatima Barnawi, who threw a bomb in an Israeli cinema, and women such as Laila Khalid, who became a legend not only among Palestinians but also among women throughout the Third World – these are exceptions, not the norm. While exceptions may indicate the beginning of women's full participation, they may also give rise to an illusionary perception that women have gained equality in the movement. The three dimensions of analysis of women's situation noted earlier in this way become more apparent. The struggle demands the unity of the sexes but there is no equality in this unity. Both inside and outside the movement, political awareness far outstrips social consciousness; the patriarchy that dominates the social system also shapes the political structure of the movement. Consequently the role of women in the movement is generally seen as the support of the *fidayin*, the freedom fighters. In order not to disrupt power relations between men and women, the movement plays safe by encouraging women to serve the struggle in their socially acceptable role – as mothers preparing their sons to fight and as wives producing fighters for the 'cause'. Women are caught in a trap where they have to find a balance between challenging their subordinate position and political exigencies which demand upholding the same cultural values in the interests of national integrity which restrain women from participating in the movement.

The subordinate position of Palestinian women in the movement is further shaped by the movement's class structure. The military, political/diplomatic and administrative wings of the movement have evolved into complex organizational modules. A new breed of educated Palestinians that constitutes the aspiring middle-class, active in the movement, along with members of old prestigious families, form the hierarchy. Their leadership is patriarchal in nature which, to a certain extent, favours women's participation; especially, of women from the same social groups who themselves have attained higher educational qualifications. The decisions to set priorities for, and policies regarding, participation of women remain in the hands of male members of the movement. The participation of women even in the most radical faction, the PFLP (Popular Front for the Liberation of Palestine) is subject to male domination. It mainly involves working on women's projects, or domestic support for the revolutionaries (producing children, arranging social activities and so on). Inasmuch as the leadership sets its political goals for women in correspondence with the social system, women's participation remains contingent upon their social position. Therefore, as Peteet (1982; 23) observes: ' . . . with slight modifications, traditional forms and mechanisms of patriarchal control continue to govern women's behaviour within the resistance'. This situation seems to have changed over the years, in the sense that, whereas in the past the structural mechanism was set to organize women separately and impose strict control on men-women relations, now women have more freedom of movement.

However, in contemporary political activism only the forms of control have changed; the constraints in themselves have not disappeared. Physical control and segregation of sexes are replaced by verbal ridicule. For example, female activists who interact with men are looked upon with contempt and named as 'loose women'. Women often encounter intimidation from male members when they try to raise women's issues, since these are not considered 'political' and are regarded as trivial. Thus most women either find it difficult to continue their political involvement, or content themselves with the secondary roles available to them. This obviously reflects the attitude of the majority of male members who consider the women's role as associated with home and domestic affairs. It explicates the third dimension of analysis noted earlier, that non-participation of women in the movement is mainly due to social constraints.

While the political participation of women is impeded as shown above, at the same time political oppression itself and the question of national liberation provide no impetus to any radical transformation of their social position. On the contrary they reimpose socio-cultural traditions, and therefore an autonomous women's movement which is likely to challenge social control is discouraged. Although such a challenge is expected to lead to the increasing participation of women in the movement, it is certainly not acceptable to the majority of male members. Therefore either the leadership of the movement does not consider it, or it has secondary status as the women's role itself. Another argument put forward for an autonomous women's movement being unnecessary within the contemporary national struggle is that through participation in the revolutionary struggle women's status will change (Fanon, 1967). However, in the case of the Algerian revolution the conclusive evidence is that: 'Algerian people battled for national independence, not especially to create a different society'. (Minces, 1978; 163)

Women's experience has been that national liberation movements, while disallowing or at the least discouraging a women's autonomous movement that could accelerate their full political participation, themselves recruit women for mass mobilization. However, when these movements successfully gain their national independence, women are conveniently pushed back into the domestic sphere. Thus women participants very correctly realize that: 'It is easier to eliminate the colonial bourgeois influences that were imposed upon us and identified with the enemy than to eliminate generations of traditions from our own society' (Davies, 1983; 131).

It is in this context that, when we look at Palestinian women's participation in the national liberation movement, despite their political awareness and their pragmatic strategies which ascribe priority to the national struggle, an alternative image of future Palestinian society in which women would not have to wage their own battle after the liberation does not emerge. Instead, while the movement itself is male dominated, women participants come mainly from bourgeois and educated middle-class groups. Some of these women even reach positions of responsibility, perhaps as UN observers, as representatives of educational institutions and so on. Some women have achieved higher positions as academics and researchers contributing to the dissemination of information about the Palestine problem to the outside world. According to 1980 statistics, women's participation in various institutions of the movement is as follows:

Table 2. Participation of Palestinian Women in PLO Institutions

Institutions	%
Steadfastness	67
(Leadership)	27
Media	24
Social Affairs	65
Palestine Red Crescent	70
(Leadership)	25
Research	45
Planning	36

Source: Samad 1986

Although these figures depict Palestinian women's involvement in many areas of the movement, such involvement has not yet reached ordinary women, especially women living in refugee camps and peasant women who have been going through the upheaval of proletarianization. Education has become a great asset to middle-class women in becoming involved in the struggle while keeping a balance between tradition and political activism. The movement certainly benefits from this state of affairs. While women cadres are critical of women's position and the role in the movement, their welfare work among ordinary women – for example in literacy classes, vocational training in sewing, typing, hair-dressing, education on nutrition, health and child-care – gives them the satisfaction of having a role in the movement. There is no denying that all these programmes are essential to the quality of life of people even under occupation, and it is necessary to have these programmes and projects to allow the movement to continue its struggle. However, they merely serve to perpetuate women's so-called extended domestic skills. Furthermore, by extending political activism to domesticity the movement has helped to sustain the gender-based division of labour between men and women. Women's participation in the movement has unquestionably influenced their lives and position. Nonetheless, the degree of change in its unevenness is highly debatable. Most importantly, female participation is conditioned by the structure and social ideology of the movement and therefore does not reach women at the popular level; and whenever it does, as we have seen, it takes the form of domesticity reaching into the political arena.

In terms of female participation, in national liberation movements that are known to have followed the same strategy whereby women are inspired to join and even recruit into the movement but where women are used as a vehicle of mobilization and in supportive roles, mere participation does not necessarily lead to equality and emancipation. Moreover, asymmetrical gender relations are not challenged even within the movement and therefore no radical transformation in the division of labour occurs. As a result, a small number of women gain some equality or challenge social control as individuals, and may even become successful, but this is not the norm. Palestinian women are no exception. Not only that; their commitment to domesticity has not challenged the unequal gender relations – they have in fact legitimized women's reproductive role and domesticity and men's exclusion from it by engaging in the domestic sector for political purposes. By giving national and patriotic meaning to women's reproductive and domestic roles without any prospect for gender equality, Palestinian women may be actually helping the patriarchy to further institutionalize gender-based division of labour and social control.

Nevertheless, it must be emphasized that there can be no doubt of the political awareness existing among Palestinian women. Whether living in the diaspora or confronting soldiers and settlers in the Occupied Territories, Palestinian women are conscious of the dialectical nature of their struggle – in other words, both the political struggle for national liberation and the need to bring social change within the society in order to extend their contribution in the national struggle.

Notes

1 The Balfour Declaration: Palestine should be re-constituted as the national home for Jewish people.
2 The Jewish claim that God promised that they would return to the promised land reinforces the legitimacy of the colonization of Palestine.
3 Some families have become refugees several times over: the first time in 1948 at the time of the establishment of the State of Israel; then in 1967 after the June War; in 1972 at the time of the PLO defeat in Jordan and in 1982 after the Israeli invasion of Lebanon.
4 Female university students have mostly been actively involved; they enjoy more freedom and opportunity for organizational activities.
5 These are the only organizations allowed by the occupation authorities.
6 In an interview with the secretary of the WWC (Working Women's Committee) in Bethlehem, I was told how proud women are to have won this holiday on International Women's Day. The secretary herself has a master's degree in biochemistry from Moscow University, lives in the Dheisheh camp and is extremely proud of serving the women's cause and being part of resistance.

References

1 N. Al-Helou and K. Lends, 'Women's Activism in the West Bank' *Al-Fajr*, 7 March 1986
2 M. Davies, *Third World, Second Sex*, Zed Press, 1983
3 F. Fanon, *A Dying Civilization*, Pelican Books, 1970
4 Y. Haddad, 'Palestinian Women: Patterns of Legitimacy and Domination' in K. Nakhleh and E. Zureik (ed.) *The Sociology of the Palestinians* London 1980
5 R. Giacoman, *Palestinian Women and Development in the Occupied West Bank*, Birzeit University Working Paper
6 J. Minces, 'Women in Algeria', in L. Beck and N. Keddie (eds.) *Women in Muslim World*, Harvard University Press, 1978
7 J. Peteet, 'No Going Back: Palestinian Women in Lebanon', *MERIP*, Jan.-Feb. 1986
8 R. Sayigh, 'Encounter with Palestinian Women Under Occupation', *Journal of Paletine Studies*, vol. X no. 4 1981
9 UN Reports *World Conference to Review and Appraise the Achievements of the United Nations Decade of Women: Equality, Development and Peace*, Nairobi, Kenya, 1984; *Palestine Statistics*, published by PLO Office, Syria, 1980; *Administered Territories Statistics* Quarterly, Israeli Central Bureau of Statistics, vol. xi, 1981, Jerusalem

Laila al-Hamdani

A PALESTINIAN WOMAN IN PRISON

WE DIDN'T ASK who had planted it, but within ourselves we all knew that this beautiful jasmine tree had been here before the state - which had built this prison - was planted on our land.

The tree was the only speck of colour in the grey surroundings, a spot of light in the darkness of our days here; that may have been the reason why they suddenly decided to cut it down. Our hearts sank with every blow of their axes on the thin, strong trunk. When our tree finally gave way, falling down and scattering its white flowers and green, delicate leaves on the ground, we watched with tearful eyes as they dragged its now dead body out of the prison yard. We wondered how a jasmine tree could be a danger to security in this prison, this state. We must have stood there a long while, speechless, staring at the empty space on the grey wall, when one of the comrades said in a clear voice, 'Well, sisters, the thing they forget is that trees have roots.' We went back to our cells, back to the daily routine, quietly smiling, knowing that it wouldn't be long before the small, green buds would rise from the ground again.

I don't know why this episode keeps coming to mind when I think about my days in prison. Maybe because it meant a lot - not only to me, but for all the girls who were there that day. It means there is always hope, even in the darkest hours of prison, and that we have the power to survive, to learn and to fight.

It all began with a little piece of paper that said that I was wanted for questioning by the military authorities. I even can't remember whether it came by post or whether it was delivered by hand, but this piece of paper determined my life for the next few years. The rest of the group to which I belonged, including my brother, had already been arrested five months previously, and so I'd spent this whole period waiting for the knock on the door at dead of night. (They don't like arresting us in broad daylight.) The darkness meant fear and pain, the vulnerability of anticipating what must come.

I was not arrested, because they assumed that I would panic and lead them to other members they did not know of. For five months I slept with my clothes on, wondering whether each night would be *the* night. At long last they gave up hope, and I was called in for questioning on the same day that the trial of my comrades began. All sorts of thoughts went through my mind and, I must confess, so did fear. What I was about to face might be anything: maybe questioning and harassment – for this has become a common experience for many of us living under occupation. On the other hand, it could also mean torture and imprisonment, as happened to one of my colleagues at university; he went in for questioning and he never came back.

My brother's face came to my mind, thin and pale, the way he looked when I visited him in prison. 'Prison is a school', he used to say, smiling cheerfully. I always wondered why they were so cheerful, so confident, when I went to see him and the others. I only came to understand this when I was imprisoned myself. Up to that point I felt they were more confident, less worried than those of us left outside.

Names echoed in my memory, names of women political prisoners who were still in prison and unable to tell of their experience. This added to my confusion. I knew that many of them were tortured, and this knowledge certainly did not make things easier.

Maskobiya

MASKOBIYA. The name still makes many prisoners and ex-prisoners shudder. That was the place I was to be interrogated in. This big, yellow-walled building, built almost a century ago by the Russian Orthodox Church, was the centre of torture stories for Palestinian prisoners. Its dark and narrow corridors and its small cells were the terrain on which many human struggles for survival have been fought, struggles to retain your honour and your sanity, in the face of a sophisticated machine of torture, designed to break you down.

As you pass through the first of the huge gates and hear it squeak closing behind you, you can't help feeling 'creepy'. You remember what people say about the place: 'The one who enters is lost; the one who gets out is reborn'. I was in now, being led to one of the many cells along an interminable corridor. It seemed to take forever, I was full of fears. Fears of the unknown.

Sounds. Sounds without images, penetrating through the thick walls, twisting around the labyrinth of corridors, rising from the cellars. The sounds were not difficult to work out. The noise of crying, of bodies being kicked, thrown against the walls, falling under blows, collapsing into the bliss of unconsciousness. The sounds of torture must be similar the world over; I learned to listen in a completely new way. I kept wondering – was it planned this way? It meant that torture was shared out between the one being tortured and the many listening ears; that every time one of us was led through these corridors of pain, we suffered with our unseen friends, hidden somewhere within this monstrous building. This kind of preparation for your own interrogation is planned to break the toughest prisoners even before the questioning starts. A kind of warning that unless you cooperate, your fate will be similar.

A small room, at the end of that awful corridor. One desk, three interrogators. On entering, it was not fear that filled me, but anger. That first session lasted for a few hours. It began with ordinary questions about my life and studies, and ended by them making it clear that I was here to stay. The noises penetrating through the walls during my questioning, made it impossible to concentrate on anything – shouting, screams, yelling and cursing. After a while I was ordered to sit facing the wall. I could sense the presence of someone in the room. I turned my face to see who was there and a sharp woman's voice ordered me: 'Keep your face to the wall, Arab bitch, and don't move.'

I could still hear the sound coming through the wall I was facing: the blows on a human body. It sounded as if the prisoner was in the middle of the room, being kicked from one torturer to another, his hands handcuffed behind his back and blindfolded, unable to avoid the next blow or to know where to anticipate it. Was this the way they killed Muhammad Abu Aker during his interrogation? What else was awaiting him, in the next room? Perhaps the hot and cold bath treatment. They knew that a man's body cannot survive a whole night in the cold bath, in the middle of winter. He was too old. They found him dead the next morning. They were very fond of using that particular method of torture – it leaves no incriminating marks on the victim's body. Sitting there, in that room, just sitting and listening, filled me with horror. My mind heaved with wondering: What? When? Is this what I will have to face? My spinal cord shrank as if under cold water; I began to sweat, feeling as if thousands of tiny creatures were creeping under my skin.

The door opened. It was time. I was taken out of the room, led down corridors, more corridors, up the stairs and more corridors. The questions in my mind got bigger and bigger. What if I could not take the torture; if they tried to rape me; what if . . . ? The faces of my family came into my mind, and the faces of my comrades in prison. Tears came to my eyes. I wondered about the man in the torture room downstairs. What was his name? What does he look like? What were the charges against him? Thinking about him was a way to quell my own fears, to hold back the tears.

All along the corridor of cells I heard: 'Be brave, sister.' Voices, faces, trying to console me. 'Be strong, comrade, don't worry. Don't let them frighten you,' the bruised faces were saying, smiling at me from behind the bars. Swollen hands were extended out, greeting, touching and encouraging. I was not alone. They must have been through inhuman torture, yet they felt the need to comfort and encourage me. I felt my fears melting away. They cannot break us.

Pushed into a cell, the door closing behind me, I heard a warm voice welcoming me. An old woman wearing the traditional embroidered dress, smiling at me. 'Don't be afraid,' she said, 'I am Umm Sabir. I was arrested three months ago.' She asked about my arrrest, and I told her everything that happened to me that morning, even about my fears.

Umm Sabir told me her story. 'I have been here three months. I still don't know what is going to happen to me. They say I killed my husband, but I didn't, I swear I didn't. They killed him. They found his body in a well by the settlement, the settlement which was built on our land. We were about to appear in court and show the documents that prove that the land belongs to us, so they killed him, and arrested me. I've only been interrogated once since then; I am still waiting. Why did they have to kill him, a poor old man, over seventy he was; wasn't it enough that they took our land and left us nothing to live on?' She started to cry and all the tears that I had held back that day streamed down my cheeks.

For the next few days, not much happened. Umm Sabir and I spent the time exchanging stories, listening to the prison sounds – dogs barking, more shouting, and sometimes the sound of men singing, a few cells away. I started singing with them. To my amazement singing filled me with hope, because I knew what these men must have been through, and I thought: 'They can still sing; not all is lost.' I started looking forward to hearing their voices and singing with them.

The next interrogation took place a week after the first one. This time I was not afraid, again encouraged by the greetings as I went down the corridor, passing the men's cells. I was prepared for the worst.

What happened was not at all what I expected. I was treated to a lecture that lasted two hours, while the interrogator spoke about the historical rights of the Jews to our land; that land actually belonged to them; that we were a bunch of Beduin who came from Saudi Arabia; and that we'd best leave this place and go where we belong.

The next chapter of this lecture dealt with the persecution the Jews suffered in the fifteenth century in Spain; then Hitler; and now the PLO and us terrorists trying to drive them into the sea. This bizarre session of mixed-up history and Zionist propaganda continued, while I listened to the dogs barking outside. 'Are you listening to me?' shouted the interrogator, his face getting redder. I was wondering – do they use the dogs to torture prisoners?

'Anyway,' the interrogator said, 'I don't expect you to become a Zionist after listening to me. I just wanted you to understand.' Understand, understand what? He did not tell me and I did not ask.

I was taken back to the cell. In the corridor, again passing by the men's cells, I felt a hand press something into mine. I couldn't work out who, of the faces looking at me through the bars, had given me it. Back in the cell with Umm Sabir, I unrolled the little piece of paper and found a song, written in pencil. Its words were simple. It said:

We are not going to die; we are
going to uproot death from our land . . .
There, far away, the soldiers will
take me, to be locked in the darkness
In the hell of chains . . .
But now I am amongst my comrades
adding my voice to theirs, now I
am strong, I can break down the
walls of my cell . . .
And I swear there will be no peace
until our revolution, our struggle
for freedom is victorious.

I learned the words by heart and joined the comrades from the men's block in singing it. It is strange, almost mysterious, the way that sharing makes one so much stronger. When I was first brought in, I felt so small and isolated, I could easily have been crushed. Now, hearing my own voice singing in unison with the others, I felt completely different. I had the strength to bring down the walls of my cell. Sharing was the first lesson I have learnt–the knowledge that behind the wall there is someone prepared to grit their teeth and ignore their pain, so as to offer you a smile of encouragement. You are not alone; thousands have passed down the same corridors before you. Harassed, tortured, even died in this place, all for the cause. It matters little that I did not know their names, they are part of you, you are part of them; that feeling of comradeship joins you together. You lose the boundaries of your own body, it becomes part of this huge, strong, living entity–you cannot help feeling the pain of their bruises on your own face.

Neveh Tirtzah

THE PARTING from Umm Sabir and the comrades in the men's cell was a tearful one–I was being transferred to Neveh Tirtzah, the women's prison in Ramleh. I only had seconds to say goodbye to everyone as I was dragged down the corridor for the last time, squeezing as many hands as I could. They will stay there, to face more torture, or will be released, or transferred to other prisons, their guilt automatically assumed. Under the Israeli legal system in the Occupied Territories, we are all guilty until proven innocent and your innocence very much depends on the political situation at the time and the mood and personalities of the interrogators. For them, each case is a professional challenge to their training and their ego, so many of them are prepared to do anything, no matter how inhuman, to get a confession from a prisoner. How many prisoners have 'confessed' to acts they have never committed, just to stop the torture, while others ended up crippled for life, some even died, rather than confess?

I had no idea what it was like in the women's prison, and my thoughts were wandering as I sat in the military jeep, handcuffed and blindfolded and surrounded by military police. Are the women allowed books? Visitors? Are they allowed contact with the outside world, or are conditions just as bad as at the detention centre, where even your lawyer is not allowed in while you are under interrogation? Though I knew that transfer to Ramleh meant that I was getting a longer imprisonment than I had expected, I was looking forward to meeting all the women I had heard so much about over the years–heroines, freedom fighters, strong women who had given up everything for the cause.

Once I was inside the prison, my blindfold was removed, as were the handcuffs. The men gave my papers to the women guards and left. While

I was changing into prison uniform, I was treated to another 'educational' session, with the guard telling me that none of this would have happened if I just stayed at home, got married and had children, instead of getting involved in stupid politics which would lead me nowhere but prison. The lecture was delivered in English, as she knew I did not speak Hebrew and she either did not speak Arabic, or preferred to speak English. Another guard then took me over to the Palestinian women's block. Going through the double gates, I saw them in their green prison uniforms, cleaning the yard and the corridors. As soon as they saw me, they all gathered around shaking my hand, hugging and patting my shoulders, with words of welcome. They then followed me down the long corridor to the cell, where the guard locked me in. I was hardly given a chance to look at my new surroundings – the women gathered at the small window in the door and showered me with questions. My name, the charges against me, news from outside – I could barely answer them all, I was so overwhelmed by the warmth of their welcome, linking me to those women who were separated from me by the heavy metal doors.

I wished I could embrace all those faces with my eyes, carve them into my heart, fearing that the minute I turned my face away, they would disappear, leaving me alone in that cell.

Then came the meetings with women I had heard of for years. The first was a strongly built woman – I realized I was looking at the first woman to be involved in the armed struggle in the Occupied Territories. She was the first to be jailed and was sentenced to a life-term plus ten years. Looking at her face, it was not difficult to imagine how she had suffered – she had been in prison eight years by then – yet she still smiled and made jokes.

The other one was a woman with magnificent eyes and a comforting, friendly smile. I had heard about her torture before I came to prison – she was sentenced to *two* life-terms plus ten years . . . How much did she have to struggle within herself, to forget or put aside the memories of torture and to keep that smile? When I heard later about the torture she suffered, I realized why she was always busy; she never allowed herself a moment of rest. I do not believe that anyone will be able to forget such a nightmare – she was beaten to the point of unconsciousness, then raped with a truncheon. She does not talk about her experiences and I deeply regretted the one time I asked her about it. It was like reopening a deep wound that took too long to heal. My questions were scratching her memory with a knife of pain, bringing back things which she had struggled to push away into the dark corners of her mind.

It is still painful to me to write about yet another story of torture. Nonetheless, these stories have to be told – so that they may not happen again; so that people know the sufferings that our women, our men, and our children have gone through and are still going through; so that the cynical phrase 'Humane Occupation' can be exposed as the cruel lie it always was.

Writing these lines, I have in mind a small, thin, sharp featured woman. She always kept herself apart, as if surrounded by a deep sadness. When I met her, I knew that here was someone who would not, who could not, compromise. During her torture, she and her father were made to strip naked in front of each other; then they ordered her father to rape her. When they both refused to comply, they had to face the most inhuman tortures.

These stories and many others were living with me, with all of us in our cells. The cell I found myself in was a small room with three bunk beds and extremely thin mattresses. It had a small window looking onto a green yard (which later I found was not allowed us) a toilet and shower cubicle, all very clean – a credit to the women who were living there. This was to be my new home. For how long?

I was allowed one hour in the prison yard, which I happily welcomed. After being locked up in Maskobiya for eighteen days, it was my first chance to talk to the women. Sitting on the ground, they were telling me about life in the prison, when we heard a scream. It was more like a wounded animal squealing. We saw a woman being dragged by three guards, her whole body was bloodstained. Despite their number she managed to free herself from them, trying in vain to escape; the place was surrounded by so many fences and masses of barbed wire . . . at last they caught her and dragged her, beating her, into a small building. I was later told it was the isolation block.

My face must have reflected the horror I felt at this display of brutality, for my friends told me that the woman was a drug addict. Unable to afford to buy the drugs from prison pushers, she would cut herself with anything sharp she could find, and became uncontrollable. 'Why don't they take her to hospital?' I asked. They told me that taking her to hospital would mean informing the prison governor, getting a special vehicle and guards – it was easier to lock her in the isolation block and get the prison nurse to stitch her up. I gathered that this happened quite often, depending on the number of drug addicts kept in the other wing of the prison. I thus learnt the prison had two wings – one for the Jewish women, mainly drug addicts, thieves and prostitutes; the other one for the Arab women, all but two of whom were political prisoners. We were not allowed into their yard, which was the patch of green I saw from my window. Only during work were we allowed to mix with the Jewish women. All sentenced prisoners had to go out to work; sometimes they also allowed those awaiting trial to work. As those that did not go to work were only allowed out for one hour per day, we all preferred to work, even though we had no choice about the kind of work we were given to do.

For work done in prison we used to get paid such meagre wages, we must have been some of the world's worst paid workers. It was not enough for the most basic needs, such as cigarettes. In addition to the wage, each of us was allowed a small sum in support from our families, to supplement our wages. Many had no families, or came from very poor ones and could not get any money from the outside. To solve this basic inequality we set up a 'common fund' into which money was put by those that could afford it and from which all our needs were met communally. This 'canteen for all' project was most successful and brought us all closer together.

The first job I was given was making clothes pegs. In the workshop building there were a number of sewing machines, and the other women told me that they had first been ordered to sew military uniforms, but had refused. This led to them being locked up for a long time, at the end of which they ended up making prison uniforms. Making clothes pegs was the most boring part of our day: sitting for six hours constantly doing the same movement really puts your brain to sleep. From the start, I decided to let my hands do the movement and to let my mind wander, think, imagine – I learned to separate mind and body. This way my mind could leave the prison, visit my family and friends, or even wander into the men's prison, separated from ours by a wall and an ever-closed gate. This gate was only used in emergencies – when they needed the male guards to beat us up, fire teargas at us, or drag a whole number of us to the isolation block, as happened when we went on strike.

To make time work for us, the Palestinian women decided to allocate daily subjects for discussion, so that each of us would prepare one, teaching the rest. This was very successful, until the Jewish women working with us complained that we were disturbing their peace and quiet, and the guards enforced total silence once again.

At the same workbench there were a couple of Jewish women, a mother and daughter. We noticed that they hardly spoke Hebrew, indeed they hardly spoke at all. We then found out they were new immigrants from the USSR, who had left everything behind and come to the land of milk and honey. They found themselves living in barrack-like dormitories with no prospect of a job, or meaningful life. In their frustration, they had beaten up a social security office clerk and now found themselves working side by side with us. Another similar woman found it impossible to live outside. When her prison term was over, she would refuse to leave; she had nowhere to go – no family, no job, no other friends, nowhere to live. She used to sit outside begging the guards to let her in, and then would go to steal, or assault someone, so as to be sent back inside. She and some of the other Jewish women were visited every day by a special sewing teacher; the hope was that this training would turn them into useful members of society.

I then realized that most of the Jewish prisoners were women from the Sephardi community, originating in the Arab countries; only a small minority came from the USSR and the rest of Eastern Europe. The relationships between us and them were quite friendly, including some petty trading, such as bartering tea for cigarettes. At break times they would separate themselves from us. We kept away from their fights unless they became too violent or dangerous. They even would use us as arbiters in their quarrels, sometimes, telling us stories about each other. This came in handy during the strike, when all privileges were withdrawn, and we were not allowed to use the prison canteen. Soon we ran out of supplies of coffee, tea and cigarettes. Two of us persuaded the Jewish women that we were able to read their fortunes in the coffee-cup, in return for supplies. As we heard so many stories about each of them from her friends and enemies, the readings were reasonably accurate, and our supplies kept flowing . . . Other services we performed for them included writing to their boy friends, as most of them were illiterate. This even led to a Hebrew class being opened for the Jewish girls, to teach them basic language skills. We were allowed to attend, and a whole number of us studied Hebrew that way. The class was wound up when the Jewish girls stopped attending – it then looked as if the class was run mainly for us, and they closed the class. Most of them came from very large families and were quite bitter about their real chances in life. They explained that anything worthwhile was in the hands of Ashkenazi (Western) Jews, and how they and other Sephardis were treated as second-class citizens. Their bitterness towards this oppression was such, that when an Ashkenazi school teacher was brought in for some crime she committed, she was totally rejected by the other Jewish women, and she ended up with us, in our section. They never missed an opportunity to kick her, especially when they found out she enjoyed some privileges denied to them – she was allowed not to wear prison uniform, and was treated much better by the guards, who, ironically, were mainly Sephardis. All this was quite new to me. Of course, I have read about the exploitation of the Sephardis in Israel, but experiencing this in prison helped us to realize that the myth of a coherent, united and strong Israeli nation was flawed at the very centre of its existence, its racist features extending beyond the Palestinians towards the whole Sephardi community, in a structure of disadvantage resembling the hated apartheid system.

The most pleasant distraction from our hateful routine was the presence of a number of children, even babies, within the walls. One of the Arab women, sentenced for murder, was pregnant when she was brought in. She had a little daughter aged two, a lovely baby, who came into prison with her and soon became a plaything for all of us. We taught her to walk, talk, eat her food – there was no shortage of volunteers to look after her . . .

One of our comrades, who had been arrested together with her husband for belonging to a guerrilla group, was also pregnant when they brought her in. Her husband was kept on the other side of that big wall, in the men's prison, and obviously he wasn't allowed to see her. He was not even told when his wife was taken to hospital to give birth. In hospital, she was in the same room with a Jewish prisoner also about to have a baby. She told her that, whether it was a boy or a girl, she had decided to call her baby 'Falasteen' – Palestine. The Jewish woman then decided to call hers Israel . . .

When she came back with her newborn baby, we all flocked to see her, only to find that the Registrar refused to record the name 'Falastin' as the boy's name. A long argument ensued, in which she made it clear that she refused to register her son under any other name. At last the Registrar gave in and registered the boy. The Jewish woman called her son David (without, one presumes, opposition from the prison authorities . . .). Little Falastin had more than fifty mothers, all competing for his attention, more than ready to play with him, feed him, sing him songs and even wash his nappies . . .

Nablus

FINALLY, four months after my arrest, it was the day of my trial. I was driven to the military court in Nablus, where, apart from my close family, the only audience were the guards. I was disappointed, as I hoped to see my friends there – as a result of a last minute change, I had been taken to a different court, and my lawyer only managing to let my family know.

I was quite confident – I assumed that I would be released either immediately, or in a month or two, because up until then, most of the Palestinians convicted on the same charge of 'membership of a banned hostile organization' had been sentenced to periods between six months and a year. To my surprise, the judge, a military officer, announced a sentence of three years, basing it on the fact that I expressed no signs of regret or repentance. It was a deterrent sentence – a warning to women that might contemplate the same course of action. I heard my mother draw in her breath, as she tried hard not to cry.

It was a cold winter day in February when I was taken back to Nablus prison. I spent ten long days in a cubby hole between the guard's toilet and washroom, as there were no other facilities for women in this prison, which was normally only used for men. I tried hard to calm down, to get used to the idea that I was to spend three years in prison. I kept thinking about people that had been sentenced for life; others that had died in prison. Compared with them, I thought, I have little to complain about. I started thinking of ways of using this time positively, so as not to be destroyed by it. I could even continue my university degree study, if they'd let me . . . I'd have to work out quite a tight schedule of work . . . By the time I was brought back to Neveh Tirtzah, I had got used to the idea that I was to spend two years and eight months in jail, with no possibility of reprieve.

Our daily timetable was unchanging and very tight; it needed all of us to maintain it. After work we had lunch, and the study period would start. It was a long struggle before they would agree to supply us with a blackboard, and later some text books. Every one of those books could tell a story of the pleading, the strikes and the bitter struggle we had to wage, to get anything at all.

One of us was teaching English; another mathematics; a third comrade taught us Hebrew, as the Hebrew classes had been terminated some time previously. She came from the part of Palestine occupied in 1948, and spoke fluent Hebrew. One of my students was Umm 'Abdalla, a seventy year-old woman. She had been arrested for feeding her son, a freedom-fighter. The official charges were – 'hiding and feeding an enemy, not informing the appropriate authorities of his and his associates' whereabouts'. She preferred to go to jail rather than inform on her son and his comrades. We were afraid that she would die in prison, she was so frail and old. After four months with us she was released, able, for the first time in her life, to write her own name and read a little. It seems that the prison authorities were worried as well – they could not afford having this old woman die in prison.

As there were a number of old women who were illiterate, we opened a special class for them. One of the women in the class was Umm Ahmad, whose son was serving a life sentence; she herself had been arrested while crossing from Jordan. She was a courageous woman, always ready with good advice; she was a mother to us all – we would rest our heads on her lap to seek comfort. She advanced well with her studies, and I was extremely happy and proud that I had come to know her.

After two hours of study, we would all go out into the yard for physical training. We all loved that part of the day, running and jumping – it was vital that we kept fit. After dinner, we would start our political education sessions. As these were not permitted, we had to post guards to keep watch for any prison guards approaching. When the doors were locked at 8 o'clock, we would read, talk and prepare for the next day's lessons.

This very active daily schedule kept us sane and healthy, much better than sitting passively, trapped in our memories of our loved ones and missing all the things we were deprived of outside. We saw what happened to most of the Jewish convicts in the other block – their time was spent in petty quarrels and crying. Sometimes the routine was broken by film shows, mainly educational films about health and childbirth. But the break was not always welcome – they kept showing us films about the first Zionist pioneers in Palestine and, again and again, films about the Holocaust and Jewish suffering – as if we were responsible for the holocaust. This forced viewing was a kind of psychological torture, totally unfair, we felt. On those occasions, our relationship with the Jewish women would suffer badly: they would begin behaving like patriots and ultra-nationalists, looking for an enemy to pick a fight with, and of course, there we were – enemies of their state, as they saw it. On one of those occasions, a Jewish girl who was normally very mild and even-tempered, stood up and shouted that the Jews should do to the Arabs what had been done to the Jews in Europe. She was usually peaceful and nice to us, but these films were stirring her violence against us.

The Israeli Day of Independence was a day of celebration for them; we would stay locked in our cells, as punishment for our hunger-strike, which was not just a protest against our own imprisonment, our individual lack of freedom, but protest against the lack of freedom of our whole nation. For us it was a day of deep grief, a day on which our agony started. For them, it marked the end of the diaspora; for us, the beginning of our own diaspora, with no end in sight. On the day the state of Israel was declared, our identity as Palestinians was denied. Could there be two groups more polarized?

For daring to stage a hunger-strike on the day of their celebration, we had to face all kinds of threats, abuses and attacks. As the day progressed, both the guards and the Jewish inmates would attack us, trying to provoke us. Our policy in the face of all this aggression, was to stay calm and not to be provoked – any reaction from our side would have led to even more aggression being vented against us. The day would end with both sides totally exhausted – them with eating, drinking and singing, us with hunger and stress. A little microcosm of the relationship between the two estranged communities in Palestine.

It would normally take more than a couple of days for things to go back to some kind of normality, a few days during which both camps avoided talking to each other. This 'normality' lasted until the next religious occasion or another political upheaval. The one occasion when things took a long time to return to normal was the Entebbe raid.

On that day we were not allowed out to work; there were no newspapers and the guards were extremely hostile and aggressive towards us. It was clear that whatever had happened was very important – otherwise they would have let us go to work. The Jewish women were not allowed into our section, and only after two days of extreme tension did we find out that a military operation was taking place in Uganda. One of the women that worked in the kitchens told us. She also found out that there might be an exchange of prisoners, and that the comrades serving life sentences stood to be freed first. The news had a very dramatic effect: comrades serving life sentences were jumping up and down like little children, overcome with joy; they handed out their meagre belongings to their friends, promising to come and liberate us all soon . . . 'We will think of you, when we're having coffee in Beirut . . . ' Their various roles in the prison, such as running the library, were delegated to others; change was in the air, urgent change.

That night none of us could sleep; over-excited, we waited for the doors to open at any moment and for our comrades to be taken on their way to freedom. But in the morning we were taken to work again, with the guards cracking jokes at our expense; the radio in the workshop gave the details of how the operation had failed. It is difficult to describe the bitter disapointment we all felt, especially the ones preparing to be liberated. We fell silent, not being able to look each other in the eye, as if it was us who had failed. But our problems were only starting – a more dangerous crisis was facing us. From the other wing we heard shrill singing and hysterical voices threatening to kill us all. Provocations continued, and aggression flared in a way that was new and more frightening than before. We could hear the guards stirring it up, which added to our fears. We asked the guards to allow us not to work, as we feared clashes, but their orders were clear – everyone must go to work. There would be no incidents, they promised. That morning I was working in our kitchen. One of the comrades told me that the Jewish convicts had got knives, through the kitchen in their section. We, of course, were not allowed to use knives in the kitchen except under constant attention from the guards. It was obvious they could not have acquired the knives without the guards turning a blind eye.

We managed to pass a warning to the girls in the workshops, but could not warn those working in the prison yard (the 'meadow' as we called it). They were cutting the grass between the barbed wire fences, so as to expose any tunnels being dug. The yard had access only through a single gate, always kept locked, even when the women were working there. On that day, one of our comrades was working there with one of the Jewish convicts. All of a sudden we heard her scream. From where I was, I could not see what had happened, but I saw the girl being carried in by two comrades. She was unconscious and one of her friends was also hurt, bleeding. They then told us that a Jewish woman who was in for prostitution had tried to strangle our comrade, who was not suspecting an attack, and in any case, was not strong enough to resist. Two of the others rushed to save her, one jumping over the fence to fight the Jewish woman – releasing the girl from her grip, but cutting herself badly as she clambered over the barbed wire fence, back to our section. The guards, realizing the seriousness of the situation, then started a big search, and many knives were retrieved from the other wing.

Incensed, we pressed charges against the other woman for attempted murder. The prison atmosphere was very tense, with the governor trying to force us to drop the charges and the girl herself came many times, trying to persuade us. We called many meetings to discuss this matter, and finally we decided to drop the charges against her. We knew that if found guilty, she would end up with another five years on her sentence. It was a difficult decision. As political prisoners, this was our first chance to assert our rights, our political strength, by insisting on pressing the charges. On the other hand, we all knew what five years in prison would mean to this young, politically inexperienced woman, who had allowed herself to be swept along by the waves of hatred and incitement all around her. Would our revenge have a political echo and meaning, or would it just be a personal vendetta? After all, we couldn't hold this poor woman responsible for the occupation, the torture, the killings – she is only a tool, a victim of a situation she does not fully comprehend. In the end, we explained to her why we were going to drop the charges. We gained a friend in her, and probably many more, to whom she spoke and explained our reasons.

Imprisonment is a severe punishment, being locked up behind walls, deprived of the most precious gift, freedom – even when, in occupied

Palestine, freedom is a somewhat abstract concept. This basic injustice was heightened by the fact that we lacked even the simple amenities allowed common criminals. As we were not criminals, we were not allowed family visits; we could not be released after two thirds of our prison term, for 'good behaviour'; we had no right of appeal against our sentence. Those basic, inalienable human rights were denied us because we were not common criminals. On the other hand, we were refused the status of 'prisoners of war'-the war between us and Zionism being totally denied, in the same way that our national identity, our land, our whole entity are constantly denied by the enemy. This way, we had none of the rights of POW's-we were termed 'Security Prisoners', according to the Emergency Regulations passed by the British Mandate government in 1945 ... We were prisoners with no rights, of a nation that did not exist, in a land no longer ours, governed by the regulations of an Empire no longer in existence ...

Fighting back ...

IN SPITE of the fact that the prison was recently built (there is always a boom in prison building in Israel) the conditions were harsh. Medical treatment, if you can call it that, was very poor. Two tablets were the only medication for ailments, and prisoners would die before the authorities would agree to take them to hospital. One of our comrades was very ill, and unable to eat or move at all. When she started having difficulties in breathing, we insisted on her being taken to hospital, or at least that an Arab doctor be allowed to visit her-we had no illusion about the type of treatment she would get in the prison clinic. Quite clearly, her life was in danger. But the authorities refused to transfer.

All this happened after a long period of tension, during which we had demanded a whole number of basic rights to be restored and a number of humiliating situations to be changed. Their refusal to transfer our sick comrade became the flashpoint of our anger and frustration. A list of demands presented to the authorities was not answered or acknowledged. The list included a long catalogue of senseless atrocities, which we demanded should be stopped.

These included the repeated arbitrary searches, carried out at any hour of day or night, with all of us waiting in the yard, cold and angry. When we returned to the cells, all our meagre belongings would be scattered on the floor, trampled on and destroyed, papers and exercise books gone for censorship. We never saw anything again. Books were almost impossible to get in-the Red Cross would tell us that they supplied books according to a list agreed by the prison authorities, yet those books would not arrive and when we inquired, all we got was abuse in return. We also complained about the humiliating way that members of our families were searched on the rare occasion of an agreed visit. During such visits, a guard would sit with us noting down every word uttered during the visit by either prisoners or visitors.

As there was no response to our demands, we refused to enter into the cell block until such a response was forthcoming. The governor ordered the guards to lock five of us in the isolation cells, and the rest in their cells. This led to an all-out strike by us. Our comrade's health was rapidly failling and we started banging on the doors and windows, demanding her immediate transfer.

The answer was more violence. This time, male guards from the neighbouring prison were brought in to beat us up. It was impossible to get away from the truncheons, it was a bloody fight which we could not win.

After these events, we all decided to go on a hunger strike, as the only way of forcing them to negotiate with us. After three days, our comrades in the isolation block were released, and negotiations on the rest of our demands could start. The result was a qualified success: our comrade was taken to hospital, some of the books were returned and they promised that confiscated material would be returned – although they would not hear about stopping the searches. It took a few months for us to realize that they reneged on most of these promises.

Three of us were exiled to the Gaza prison for our role in the strike. We ended up having to wage a new battle in order to have them returned. We were not allowed to correspond with them at all. We were not successful, and slowly things went back to normal.

Time in prison has completely different qualities from the time spent elsewhere, for obvious reasons. One dreads certain times of the day, and eagerly expects others. The most special part of any day for all of us was four o'clock in the afternoon. It was then that we got newspapers, but, most important of all, letters were handed out. The guard arriving with the letters had us all standing around her with trepidation, our eyes fixed on her lips, trying to decipher the sounds of names before they were uttered. When you got a letter, the excitement was too much – you would start reading it even before you found a chair to sit down. Those of us who did not hear our name read out would quietly disperse, trying to hide the enormous sense of disappointment, the tear or two, the hope dashed but not totally given up – maybe tomorrow . . . I used to read my letters many times, learning them by heart and reciting them to myself during my long hours at work. Tenuous as they were, the letters were our main link with the outside - visits were only allowed once a month. We were allowed to write six letters a month ourselves, on very small sheets of prison-supplied paper.

When we write, we know that not only our family and friends are going to read it; there will also be the prying hands and eyes of the censor looking at every single word, decoding any hints, recording any details. Our letters could not be the intimate contact that we wished them to be, that we so needed them to be. Our friends and families outside knew the same, and remembered the same when writing to us. This feeling of being looked at through a keyhole, of your most intimate feelings being paraded naked in front of someone hostile and unknown, was one of the worst punishments in the prison system.

It was after two years in prison tht I first met Ruth. She was an Israeli sociology student from the Hebrew University, and she came to the prison often, as part of a study in criminology that she was conducting with the Israeli prisoners. When we first met, she was reluctant to speak to me; she was actually frightened of me. When she plucked up courage we ended up talking for hours. She told me she was frightened to death in our section of the prison, which she referred to as the 'terrorist' section. She had clear expectations of being physically attacked when she came in, and was surprised, even confused, by our friendly reaction.

Having overcome her fear, she started visiting us quite often. We became close friends and discussed everything, from theatre to music, to sex and family relationships. She told me about problems she had with her husband, and we talked of mutual academic interests - I was studying sociology before I was arrested. She even told me about friends of hers, to whom she planned to introduce me, after my release from prison. The guards warned her about us, about me, but this did not deter her, and she continued visiting me. For me, she had become not only a friend, but also a most welcome change in my prison routine. Warnings came from both sides, with my comrades arguing that she had been sent to spy on us, but it did not affect my determination to continue the friendship and the dialogue.

But our dialogue was not complete. One subject we both avoided totally was politics. Of course, we had to come to it sooner or later, and one day Ruth asked the fated question, 'How did you come to be here?' and then concluded with a rather naive, but moving statement about the fact that we seemed to get on with each other so well, so why fight, why not get together, put aside the conflict?

It was clear she did not see a political dimension to the conflict, so I began to talk to her about the fate of Palestine since the beginning of the

Zionist settlement, tried to describe to her the aspect of the conflict that was always invisible to her, as it still is, to most Israelis. The occupation, the destruction, loss of homes and family, of the rural and urban communities, of their cultural traditions, of their national and social sense of identity. The diaspora, one country after another rejecting us; a life with no future; a life with no constant and clear connection to a place; a landscape of home; a life of divisions and conflicts, in which disaster is a daily visitor in every family, and catastrophe is routine. I said that as a Jewish woman she should have no problem in understanding this fate of ours. Were the Jews not outcasts for centuries, refugees, victims of oppression?

She was quite shocked, crying throughout my story and saying repeatedly: 'This is not what they tell us in school; I never heard any of this before; I had no idea . . . ' A long period of heavy silence followed. Ruth was battling with herself, taking her time, she was preparing to ask me another important question. I later understood she came armed with that question, a question that she treated like a kind of political litmus paper. She broke the silence by asking: 'Suppose that one day we meet on opposite sides, me with an Uzi sub-machine gun, and you with a Kalashnikov rifle – would you be able to shoot me?'

I was quite shocked. She obviously had not understood my story (I told myself) if she could come up with this comic-strip formulation of our political and human dilemma. I told her: 'If we met in the way that you describe, on opposite sides of the front, it means that we are going to shoot at each other, because that is why we are there. I shall be fighting for my freedom; what will you be fighting for? Probably, your right to deny my freedom? In that situation, do not count on me not to shoot you. I will not wait to be shot by you, or anybody else. I will shoot first; I will try to be faster, to survive.'

We spoke no more. Suddenly I realized that there was always a barrier between us, like a glass wall, invisibly separating our positions. We pretended not to see it, we did not want to admit its existence, but we both felt it. Her question made both of us realize that as long as she was the occupier and I the occupied, as long as we were not equals we would never be able to transcend this invisible barrier.

Ruth never came back. If she was to understand, she would have had to give up too many things that she was not ready to abandon, not yet, and probably, not ever. I was sad. I felt I had not lost a friend, but gained an enemy. An enemy who might just cry while doing the killing.

This relationship with Ruth comes to my mind often, when I hear talk about 'peaceful coexistence' between the occupied and the occupier, the oppressor and the oppressed, the lamb and the wolf. The lines of the poem I first learned in prison come back, from the distance of pain:

> And I swear there will be no peace
> until our revolution, our struggle
> for freedom is victorious.

Nira Yuval-Davis

THE JEWISH COLLECTIVITY

INTRODUCTION

NATIONS, as Ben Anderson points out,[1] are imagined communities. In the case of Israel, the imagined community has been a direct product of the dreams, as well as the actions, of the Zionist movement which established the state. This does not make it any less historically real than other nations, but it might make it more historically precarious.

This article explores the ways in which the boundaries of the Israeli Jewish collectivity have been defined and reproduced, in relation to the Jewish people on the one hand and to the Israeli society on the other. Specifically, it looks at the ways in which Jewish women and childbearing have been ideologically constructed to play certain roles in the above process, and the consequent effects of this on the social and legal position of women in Israel.

The issue of national reproduction in Israel, both in terms of its ideological boundaries and in terms of the reproduction of its membership, has always been at the centre of Zionist discourse. Lately, it has gradually come to overshadow even the issue of security as a precondition for Israel's survival. An extreme expression of this position can be read in the introduction to Rabbi Kahane's book *Thorns in Your Eyes* (Kahane is the leader of the fastest growing political power in Israel, the Kakh party – a neo-Nazi party, although many, especially his supporters, see it as the most consistent of the Zionist parties). According to Kahane:

'Each Jew should ask himself the following question: I am the son of a people that wandered around without a homeland of its own for nearly 2,000 years. I am the son of a people who suffered persecutions and immeasurable holocausts, big and small. I am the son of a people that, unlike other peoples, was not allowed to develop in its body and spirit in its own country. Today, following the death of six millions and with God's help, we do have a state which embodies our sovereignty, defends itself with our army, and follows our culture. Am I prepared – in peaceful conditions and with THE ARAB RATE OF POPULATION GROWTH (*My emphasis. NY-D*) which is transforming a minority into a majority – to allow, even in a democratic manner, the change of the name of the state to Palestine; to cancel the Law of Return which entitles each Jew an automatic right of entry and citizenship (the cornerstone of the Zionist thinking on maintaining the Jewish majority), and peacefully and democratically to end the Jewish state?' [2]

It is Kahane asking the question, but he is not alone. Already Golda Meir, then prime minister of Israel, had confided in the early 1970s that she was afraid of a situation in which she 'would have to wake up every morning wondering how many Arab babies have been born during the night'! [3]

A 'demographic race' between the Jews and the Arabs in Israel is seen as crucial, then, for the survival of Israel. Israel, not as a state apparatus for the population living in it, but as the state of the Jews all around the world. Revealingly, the official aim of the Israeli demographic centre which was established as a unit attached to the Israeli prime minister's office in April 1967, was 'to act systematically to realize a demographic policy directed at creating an atmosphere and the conditions for encouraging a birth rate, which is so vital to the future of the JEWISH PEOPLE. (*My emphasis. NY-D*) [4]

More than 75 per cent of world Jewry, according to the statistics produced by that same demographic centre, live outside Israel. On the other hand, 17 per cent of Israeli citizens, and about a third of the people under the direct control of the Israeli government (including those living in the territories occupied by Israel since 1967), are not Jews. How is it, then, that the Israeli government, portrayed for so many years as 'the only democracy in the Middle East', is worried explicitly, not about the demographic future of its own civil society, but about the Jewish people?

As Kahane says, Israel was established for a specific purpose, and as an achievement of a specific political movement – Zionism. While the definition of boundaries of national collectivities and their relationship to the state is very often problematic, in Israel it is especially so, because of the specific historical construction of the Jewish people, as well as the settler colonial character of Israeli Jewish society. Exploring these issues will be the purpose of the first part of this article.

Symbolic reproduction of the Israeli Jewish national collectivity depends on the availability of people 'of the right kind' to 'man' it. One of the basic concerns of the Zionist movement, especially the Labour Zionist movement, since the beginning of the Zionist settlement in Palestine, has been the creation of a Jewish majority in the country as a precondition for the establishment of the Jewish state there. In the early period of Zionist settlement and up until the early 1960s, the major form of the supply of 'human power' to the *yishuv*, the Zionist settler society, has been by *aliyah*, the immigration of Jews to the country. Gradually, however, the objective and subjective conditions for *aliyah* have dwindled, and Israeli Jewish national reproduction has come to rely more and more on Israeli-born babies.

Demographic policies often seem to be determined by worries about the existence of sufficient labour power for the national economy, and indeed the literature on reproduction often assumes it to be the complementary facet of economic production or rather a precondition of it.[5] A closer examination of national demographic policies (as well as state welfare policies), however, will often reveal that national political rather than economic interests lie behind the desire to have more children, or rather more children of a specific origin.[6] In Israel, where economistic calculations have never seriously determined major political decisions (even today, in the heart of an extreme economic crisis[7]), this has been especially true. The second part of the article will therefore concentrate on examining the nationalist angle in the ideological debates and policies which have surrounded the question of birthrate of Israeli children.

The last part of the article will focus on the ways in which the political and ideological pressures on defining and reproducing the national collectivity in Israel have constructed and affected Israeli Jewish women as its national reproducers.

PART I
THE ISRAELI 'NATION' AND ITS BOUNDARIES

IN THE ISRAELI Declaration of Independence in 1948, Israel is defined as the Jewish state established by and for the Jewish people:

'The Land of Israel was the birthplace of the Jewish people . . . the Jewish people remained faithful to it in all the centuries of their dispersion . . . strove throughout the centuries to go back . . . In the year 1897, the first Zionist congress, inspired by Theodor Herzl's vision of the state of the Jews, proclaimed the right of the Jewish people to national revival in their own country . . . The Jewish state would open its gates to all Jews and endow the Jewish people with equality of status among the family of nations . . . On 29 November 1947, the United Nations assembly received a resolution in favour of the establishment of a Jewish state in the Land of Israel . . . this recognition of the United Nations in the right of the Jewish people to establish its own state cannot be confiscated . . . We hereby proclaim the establishment of the Jewish state in Palestine – the Land of Israel . . . '[8]

The declaration has no legal authority in Israel. (Indeed, many Israeli laws, and even more so practices, would have been declared illegal were it to be recognized as a constitutional document; among other things, the declaration also promises that the state of Israel 'will uphold the full social and political equality of all its citizens without distinction of religion, race or sex . . . ') Nevertheless it has had a symbolic importance, as representing the widest consensus of the Zionist movement which established the state of Israel. Among those who signed it are even representatives of parties like the extreme religious Agudat Israel and the Communist Party, who did not define themselves as Zionist but still provided legitimation for the establishment of Israel as a Zionist state.

There is no space here to recount in detail the history of the Zionist movement and its internal divisions.[9] Suffice it to say that the basis of its widest consensus is reflected in the Declaration of Independence, in which Israel is seen as the state of all Jews. Israel was never meant to be a political expression of its civil society, of the people who reside in its territory or even of its citizens. It was meant to be the State of the Jews, wherever they are. And in that respect it was immaterial (albeit highly inconvenient) that only 55 per cent of the population in the Jewish state proposed by the 1947 UN resolution were Jews, and they owned only about five per cent of the land there, or that even today the Jews in Israel constitute less than a quarter of world Jewry.

Last October, the Knesset, by passing what is ironically known as the 'anti-racist' law,[10] gave a more specific interpretation to the consensus expressed in the Declaration of Independence. It defined Israel as 'the state of the Jewish people', and not just as 'the Jewish state' – which Zionist liberals would have liked to believe represented the same relationship between state and nation in Israel as in any other Western country. It does not – as the rest of this section will attempt to show.

The legal expression of the relationship betwee Israel and the Jewish people has been the Israeli Law of Return (mentioned by Rabbi Kahane) according to which all Jews, wherever they come from, are entitled automatically to Israeli citizenship, while according to the Israeli Nationality Law, non-Jews, even if born in Israel, unless born to Israeli citizens (residency and settlement are not sufficient for that purpose), are not. This special relationship between the Israeli state and the Jewish people expresses itself in many other ways as well – symbolic, legal and administrative. (Not least among them is the functioning of the Jewish Agency, the executive arm of the Zionist movement, as a parallel state distributive apparatus, operating exclusively for Jews). [11]

This relationship makes the criterion according to which people are included or excluded from the category of Jew to be of central and vital importance. Subjective and cultural identification are by no means sufficient.

Who is a Jew?

THE MODERN ideological and legal debate on the definition of 'the Jew' had already started by the time of the French Revolution, when the question of the legal emancipation of the Jews came to the fore. It focused on the question of whether or not the Jews constituted a nation, or merely shared a religion. In a way, this debate has not been fully 'decided' until today – at least two Israeli governments fell as a result of disagreements on the question of 'who is a Jew' and last year the debate even shook the present Israeli government. [12]

Historically, in the Estate society of feudal Europe where 'classical Judaism' crystallized, [13] the Jewish communities, the *kehilot*, were often organized around the more or less specific economic role the Jews had as a middle caste between the landed nobility and the peasantry or the urban poor. As such, they usually had a certain degree of autonomy and self government and their religion expressed itself more as a total way of life, than as a belief in certain religious dogmas. Part of their religious culture was the tradition of a common origin and history, which included political independence before the destruction of the second Jewish Temple in Jerusalem in 70 AD. Like many other ethnic collectivities therefore, in Europe and even more so in the Third World, the dichotomy of nation/ religion has not suited the historical constrution of the Jewish people. Zionism, it is important to remember, has only been one response, and for a very long time a minority one, of the Jews in the 'modern' world to this history, and to their displacement and persecution with the rise of capitalism and nationalism in Europe, in which their traditional mode of existence could no longer survive. Hassidism and Jewish Orthodoxy on the one hand and Reform Judaism on the other hand have been the major religious movements which emerged as a reaction. Secularization and assimilation, both liberal and socialist, have been two other popular reactions by Jews to the 'Jewish problem' in the modern world.

The two large Jewish political movements in the 20th century which attempted to resolve the 'who' or, rather, 'what is a Jew' dilemma by constructing Jewishness into a nationality, have been the Jewish Bund and the Zionist movement. The Bund, which was the dominant Jewish national movement in Eastern Europe before World War II, saw the Jews there as constituting an autonomous national collectivity, with its own language and cultural tradition. They aspired for a multinational state structure in Eastern Europe in which the Jews, like all the other national minorities, would have a national and cultural autonomy. [14]

The Zionist movement aspired to the 'normalization' of the Jewish people, by establishing a Jewish state in an independent territory in which, ideally, all Jews would eventually settle. After long debates and the proposal of various alternative locations, it was decided that Palestine, which in the Jewish tradition had been the 'Land of the Fathers' and the 'Promised Land', would be the territorial basis for this state. Colonialism and exclusionary practices against the native population of Palestine have been, therefore, an integral part of the Zionist endeavour. It became historically successful due to the specific historical configuration in Europe and the Middle East post-World War I, and especially in the aftermath of World War II and the Nazi Holocaust. The physical extermination of such large numbers of European Jewry, combined with the survival of the Zionist settlers in Palestine (which the Nazis never reached), created a myth that Zionism presented a successful strategy against anti-Semitism and Israel a secure refuge for persecuted Jews. The superpowers supported this presumption of the Zionist movement, and the establishment of the Israeli state, because it was more convenient for the USA to send the postwar Jewish refugees to Palestine than to have to absorb them en masse in their own postwar societies. It was also a way for the Americans and the Soviets to penetrate the Middle East, an area which up until then had been controlled by the British and French.

As a result, the Zionist movement came to be the hegemonic movement in World Jewry. To the majority of Jews, Israel has become, at least to an extent, their *post facto* homeland. Sending money to Israel has become an easy way of being Jewish, especially for the non-religious Jews who still felt the need, especially after the Holocaust experience, to express their Jewishness. Israel has also become an emotional 'insurance' policy, as a potential refuge from persecution. (In reality, of course, Israel's very existence is dependent to a very large extent on the political and financial support of the Jewish Diaspora). Concurrently, the Establishment of the various institutions of the organized Jewish communities has become very dependent on its relations with Israel, in terms of channels of power and prestige. One of the results of this process, especially in the last ten to fifteen years, has been the dissociation of Jews, especially young Jews, who do not want to be identified as supporters of Zionism and Israel, from any association whatever with the structured Jewish community. This phenomenon, plus the high rate of mixed marriages (up to a third) among young Jews has raised a debate among demographers not only about how many Jews exist in the world, but also about who should be defined as such. In Israel itself, religious legislation has been chosen as the criterion for membership in the Jewish collectivity.

This requires explanation, as the Zionist movement has generally presented itself as a 'modern alternative' way of being Jewish, as opposed to the traditional religious one. However, in spite of the fact that the majority of Zionists were, at least originally, vehement secularists, the Zionist movement never completely broke away from Jewish Orthodoxy. The Zionist movement needed the religious tradition in order to justify its claim that Palestine was its homeland, rather than the land of its indigenous population; it also needed the recognition of at least major sections of the Orthodox Jewish communities, as the Zionist movement claimed to represent all Jews all over the world.

This is why, (in addition to more *ad hoc* government coalition calculations), there has always been a partial incorporation of Jewish religious legislation into Israel's state legislation. A central aspect of this incorporation relates to the kind of criteria whereby one can be considered a member of the Jewish national collectivity. A Jew – as defined by the law, following the traditional religious construction – is 'anybody who is born to a Jewish mother or has been converted to Judaism' (the question of which forms of religious conversion will be recognized by the state is still being debated).[15] The Israeli Law of Return, the Nationality Law and various administrative regulations use Jewishness as a criterion for entitlement to various privileges in Israel (in spite of its supposed parliamentary democratic welfare state structure), such as automatic right for citizenship, loans, housing etc.

The incorporation of the criterion of religious conversion in state legislation has created a situation in which religious conversion is used in instances which in other states would have been dealt with by simple acts of naturalization. An extreme example of this is that of the Black American Olsi Perry, a professional basketball player. He had to undergo circumcision as part of his supposed religious conversion in order to be able to play in the Israeli national team . . .

On the other hand, Jewish national ideology is explicit in placing a greater emphasis on the right 'genetic' origin than other national collectivities. A couple of years ago, there was an outcry in Israel when it was discovered that childless couples who despaired of getting babies for adoption were using the services of private American agencies to import Brazilian and Columbian babies. The outcry was that, as it was done illegally and secretly, these babies will grow up as Jews, without 'really' being so (since they were not born to a Jewish mother and had not been converted to Judaism); this will create havoc in the reproduction of the Jewish collectivity when they marry and produce children as if they are Jewish, when they are 'really' not. [16]

To be born Jewish, however, is more than purely a genetic matter. To be a Jew, one has to be born to a Jewish mother in the 'proper' way – otherwise one is considered a *mamzer* (bastard), cannot be considered a Jew, is not able even to become a Jew by conversion, and one's descendants cannot marry other Jews 'for ten generations to come'. Bastardy in Judaism is not a question of being born outside wedlock, since according to Jewish religious law sexual intercourse is one of the ways in which marriage can be contracted (as long as it is with another Jew – rapes during pogrom did not receive such a 'sanctification', but on the other hand, they are the historical reason why Jewishness has come to be defined via the mother rather than the father in classical Judaism). Bastardy is rather a question of being born to a woman who is having a forbidden relationship of adultery or incest – and that includes even women who have been divorced by civil (rather than religious) courts, which, unlike civil marriages, are not recognized by the religious court. Their children by their second husbands would be defined as bastards.

The major ideological justification which has been given for the incorporation of Orthodox religious personal law into Israeli legislation, and for accepting its definition as to 'who is a Jew', has been that doing otherwise will 'split the people'. It was claimed that accepting the authority of other Jewish religious denominations, such as Conservative or Reform Judaism, let alone secular legislation, would make it impossible for Orthodox Jews to marry anyone but other Orthodox Jews, for fear of incorporating unintentionally the forbidden *mamzers* into their family. The paradox is, of course, that in reality no Orthodox Jew would marry a non-Orthodox Jew (or even newly 'born again' Orthodox Jews who come from secular families)–exactly because of this fear. Moreover, outside Israel the majority of Jews do marry and divorce in a non-Orthodox fashion, even if they are married by a rabbi, and in Israel itself private contracts in lawyers' offices have become more and more popular as an established alternative to official marriages.[17] The attempt to control the boundaries of the Israeli collectivity and its patterns of reproduction in a homogeneous way by incorporating severe Orthodox religious law into Israel's state legislation has, therefore, not really succeeded.

All this means that the boundaries of the Jewish national collectivity which Israel claims to represent are not clear at all. On the one hand, they are definitely wider than the boundaries of the Israeli Jewish national collectivity, but on the other, there clearly exist many organized (mainly Orthodox and some Socialist) and especially unorganized segments of the world Jewish population who less and less recognize Israel's claim to represent them. Moreover, the historical past of the Jews as a religious civilization and with separate histories in different parts of the world, has presented contradictory and cross pressures on the Zionist movement when it attempts to construct the national boundaries of its collectivity without at the same time breaking radically with its ideology of religious/ethnic construction.

But contradictions in and challenges to the determination of the boundaries and nature of the Israeli national collectivity have emerged not only in relation to world Jewry outside Israel, but also in relation to divisions and struggles within it.

Internal Israeli Divisions

THE PROBLEMS concerning the nature and boundaries of the Israeli national collectivity get yet another twist when we look at the internal ethnic divisions within its Jewish collectivity, especially the major division into Occidental and Oriental Jews. Jewish communities, if only small ones, exist in most countries today, and in Israel itself there are Jews who have come to settle from over seventy countries. Historically and culturally they can be divided mainly into three major groups, Ashkenazi, Sephardi and Oriental. The Ashkenazi Jews resided in Central and Eastern Europe. Their language (in addition to the languages of their countries of residence) was Yiddish. The Sephardi Jews originated from the Jewish community in Spain (expelled in 1492) and resided mainly in Western Europe and the Mediterranean countries. Their specific langauge was Ladino. In the Arab world too, there existed Jewish communities; their language was Arabic. In Palestine, Ashkenazi Jews started to settle in significant numbers only towards the end of the eighteenth century, and Zionist settlement started only towards the end of the nineteenth century. Prior to that, most Jews in Palestine had been Sephardic.

The ideology, the leadership and the overwhelming majority of the Zionist settlers and supporters of the Zionist movement until the post-World War II period came from Europe, especially Eastern Europe, and originated from among the Ashkenazim.

The Jews from Arab countries mostly arrived in Israel after the establishment of the state in 1948. Unlike the Zionist settlers from Europe, they usually came not as single individuals but as whole families and communities. To the extent that their migration was ideological at all, it had more to do with religious beliefs than any aspiration for the social transformation of the Jewish people. Unlike most of the European Jewish communities, they were not exterminated during World War II, but their situation began to worsen dramatically with the growing conflict between the Zionist movement and the Arab world as a whole. When they arrived, the Oriental Jewish communities, as they became known collectively in Israel, came into an already well crystallized political structure, with its pre-established supporting economic underpinnings. The task of absorbing the new immigrants was given to the various Zionist parties according to their relative size in the Jewish Agency.[18] As a result of this system of patronage, the political map of Israel hardly changed in terms of its balance of power for almost the first thirty years of its existence, in spite of the very different political and economic interests held by these new immigrants, whose families came to make up the majority of the Israeli Jewish population. Autonomous Oriental Jewish parties, unlike Palestinian ones, were not forbidden by law, but (at least until the 1970s), they were just not allowed sufficient access to independent economic and political levers. Within the old party system, the national political leadership, with very few exceptions, continued to be composed of Ashkenazi Jews (especially East Europeans) and their children.

As in the case of the Palestinians in Israel, the process of change had started gradually, but would probably not have transformed itself as it did without the major shift in the Israeli society as a result of the 1967 war. The entrance en masse of Palestinian labour power into the Israeli labour market not only involved a relative upward shift for the Israeli working class, which after the 1950s was overwhelmingly Oriental; it also supplied markets and cheap labour for those among the Oriental Jews who started their own enterprises and/or engaged Palestinians as workers in their fields in the moshavim.

In spite of occasional complaints that the settlements in the Occupied Territories were diverting money from the rehabilitation of urban slums and underprivileged development towns where the majority of Oriental Jews lived, the mass of Oriental Jews came to support the Likkud party and parties even further to the Right. They saw these parties as serving their class interests, as well as satisfying their growing expressed hostility to the former dominant Labour Zionists who had acted as their controlling patrons since their arrival in Israel.[19] Even after a major economic crisis and the establishment of the national unity government, there have been no signs of significant political changes among the majority of Oriental Jews.

Their challenge, however, was not only political but also cultural. They were revolting against the under-rating and suppression of Oriental Jewish culture which had been part of their 'absorption' process – whereby modernization was equated with westernization, and Jewish nostalgia was focused on the East European Shtetl of *Fiddler on the Roof* rather than on *Our village in the Atlas mountains*.[20] The quotable Golda Meir not only lived in fear of Arab babies being born, but, it is said, also cried in relief when Russian Jews began arriving in Israel in the early 1970s: 'At last real Jews are coming to Israel again' . . .

In the last few years, however, the power struggle which has been taking place in Israel to challenge western exclusivity and supremacy concerning culture, education and power political structures, has to a certain extent got enmeshed with the power struggle of the religious sector to reinstate religious tradition as the legitimate basis for social and political action in Israel.

Soon after the 1967 war, major changes began to materialize in the centrality, saliency and intensity of various ideological trends within Israel, including within the dominant Ashkenazi establishment. These changes have had to do with changing perspectives on the relationship between being an Israeli and being a Jew – in social and political, as well as religious, terms.

The *sabras*,[21] The 'New Jews', grew up feeling themselves to be a positive alternative, and completely different, to the Diaspora Jews. After the establishment of the state, the term 'Zionism' itself became in Israeli slang a euphemism for meaningless waffle. There was a feeling (contradictory political and financial reality notwithstanding) that the Zionist movement had finished its task with the establishment of the state of Israel and the mass immigration in the first few years of its existence. There even developed ideological movements which attempted to classify the Israeli Jews as part of the ancient Semitic region in which Israel's long term future lay (without usually discarding assumptions of Israeli superiority . . .).[22] Diaspora Jews were looked at a bit contemptuously, and as an ongoing source for contributions of money given in order to salve their conscience for not having come to settle in Israel; religious Jews were looked on, to a great extent, by the dominant majority, as an anachronism left over from the 'Diaspora period'.

The 1967 war changed all that. It suddenly became clear (and even more so in the 1973 war) that Israel is actually dependent for its existence on Jewish financial and political support from outside Israel. A growing active concern for the Jewish communities abroad was the other face of the growing Israeli hegemony in the international Jewish communities. Moreover, the debate on the Occupied Territories (between those who wanted a Greater Israel which had subordinated Palestinians within it, and those who wanted an Israel which was perhaps smaller, but as far as possible 'purely' Jewish) raised again the whole discussion about the nature of the Zionist endeavour, as live an issue as is the relationship between the Jewish people and Israel.

However, the changes went deeper than that. The 1967 war, in which the Wailing Wall and the other Jewish holy places were captured, was also endowed with a religious interpretation – it was a 'miracle', the 'hand of God'. (The defeat in Lebanon was also to be seen as the hand of God – this time as a punishment for not keeping to the religious code . . .) The ideological trend which has seen the establishment of the Jewish state as a religious mission was strengthened. And this was by no means confined to religious circles. It is not incidental that after 1967 new Israeli soldiers began to swear allegiance to the army no longer on Masada,[23] a symbol of national liberation warfare, but in front of the Wailing Wall, the last remnant of the Jewish Temple; nor that by now so many kibbutzim, traditionally strongholds of secularism in Israel, have synagogues.

But the most far-reaching changes have taken place in the politics and the position of the Zionist religious sector itself. The Zionist religious parties have always been the traditional coalition partners in Israeli governments. Until 1967, they willingly accepted the Labour parties' military and international policies in exchange for economic benefits for their institutions and keeping the *status quo* on religious legislation more or less intact. After 1967, however, and especially among the younger generation, the product of religious state education, they started to develop their own political line. This focused on the issue of annexation and settlement of the West Bank and the other territories of the 'Promised Land' as a religious duty. From occupying a secondary and inferior role – both in the eyes of the dominant Labour Zionists and in the eyes of non-Zionist Orthodox Jews–they saw themselves (and were seen by others) as occupying a pioneering front-line role in Zionism and religious affairs as a whole. The rise, in 1977, of the rightwing Likkud party government was partly prompted by this process; it also accelerated it. The religious parties, Zionist and non-Zionist alike, switched their allegiance as government coalition partners from the Labour Party to those who were closer to them politically and who also gave them much larger economic resources for their specific institutions. As a result, it is claimed, Israel now has more 'Yeshiva Bokhers' (religious scholars who are kept by the community) than existed in nineteenth-century Poland. The process of settlement in the Occupied Territories, as well as the militancy of religious circles in all spheres of Israeli life, are growing all the time. The reconstitution of the Labour Party as the head of a national coalition government has not seriously affected this process. [24]

It is important to note, however, that not all the growth of the religious sector has taken place in the nationalist camp. The ideological crisis, combined with the economic crisis in Israel since the 1970s, has led many to turn to religious fundamentalism, not as a messianic, nationalistic, if not fascistic movement, (parallel to fundamentalist movements in the Muslim world) but as an escape from all the moral and political dilemmas that Zionism (which most of them see as having failed) has presented to contemporary Israeli and non-Israeli Jews (a phenomenon common to disappointed youth all over the West). Studying the Torah and keeping the Halakha seem to many, mostly Ashkenazi but also Sephardi *sabras*, as the only valid way for Judaism to continue to exist, and for them to live as Jews and to find emotional security and certainty.

The intermeshing of the power struggles of Oriental Jews and the religious Jews has meant that in Israel there is a growing body which sees western culture and values as a threat (if not as a contemptible anachronism–I did hear a student on a bus one day being teased for being so dumb as to still believe in Darwinism). Correlated to these developments is a considerable growth of an Israeli neo-fascist movement, in which the class grievances of poor Oriental Jews are combined with nationalistic religious myths, and in which democracy is seen as a trap invented by the ruling Establishment, from which only they and the Palestinians, the national enemy, can benefit.

What is challenged here, in different ways, is not so much the boundaries of the Israeli national collectivity, but the nature of the collectivity itself. Whereas at the beginning of the Zionist endeavour the dominant trend had been to create in Israel a nation state in the western mode, as 'normal' as possible within the constraints of the Zionist mode, there are now more and more voices calling for European-dominated values to be driven out of Israel, and for the country to be turned into an ethnic collectivity united by religious traditions and practices, with modern state powers to enforce and exclude others. In turn, these challenges to the nature of the Israeli Jewish collectivity affect approaches to the question of reproduction of the national collectivity itself, its relationship with world Jewry, and its attitudes towards those in Israel who are not Jews.

The Israeli National Collectivity and the Palestinians

UP TO NOW I have discussed the relationship between Israel and the Jews, both in and out of Israel. However, as I said previously, about 17 per cent of Israel's citizens are not Jewish, and the figure reaches about a third of the population when we include the people who have lived for the past eighteen years under the control of the Israeli state in the Occupied Territories. The latest statistical scare has been that last year more non-Jewish than Jewish babies were born in areas under the control of the Israeli government. [25] The overwhelming majority of those non-Jews are Palestinian Arabs.

The Palestinian Arabs 'threaten' the Zionist endeavour in more ways than one. Their presence is a continual reminder that Palestine has not been an empty country 'waiting for two thousand years for its sons to return', as the Zionist myth puts it; it is also a continual obstacle as regards reconciling the ideological constructs of a western-type welfare state (the model which Israel has attempted to follow, but in which by definition all citizens are supposed to be treated on a universal basis) with Zionism, which demands exclusive rights, or at least a privileged position, for Jews.

This contradiction remained in 'manageable' proportions until 1967, with the Palestinians constituting no more than 13 per cent of the Israeli population. Furthermore, for many years the Palestinians in Israel were made to live in relative geographical isolation. They were concentrated in two major areas – Galilee and the 'Triangle', and they almost always lived in separate settlements. Military government operated in Israel until 1965 (two years before Israel came to occupy the West Bank and Gaza strip) and this meant that Palestinians had to obtain special permission in order to travel outside their home zones. Up until the 1967 war, the Israeli Palestinians were sufficiently segregated from the Jewish collectivity, to enable the feasible operation of the Israeli state in most of its facets in a supposed universal fashion. However, even within these containments, the long term contradictions started to emerge.

The continuous pressure for expropriating Palestinian lands, both for positive reasons – to expand Jewish settlement – and negative – to prevent the emergence of excessive concentrations of Palestinian enclaves within Israel – have had the paradoxical result of integrating the dispossessed Palestinians into the Israeli labour market. The Palestinians have undergone a process of proletarianization and were incorporated as a class fraction at the bottom of the Israeli class structure, especially in unskilled and manual work in the private sector.[26]

Consequently, not only were they brought into closer social and economic interaction with Jewish society, but this change also brought more education and more money to the Palestinian villages. One result of this process, and of the numerical growth of the Israeli Palestinian population, has been a relative strengthening of their political power as Israeli citizens, especially as a voting bloc, no longer fully controllable by traditional mediators sponsored by the authorities. This has somewhat improved their collective bargaining power. Unsurprisingly, however, there is only a very small improvement in the representation of Palestinians in real political power positions, and all attempts at independent Palestinian political organization continue to be blocked.[27] Moreover, the basic apartheid-type discriminations and exclusions in the supply of amenities, state resources and supplementary benefits continue to operate, in an atmosphere in which interpersonal racism towards the Palestinians is growing all the time.[28]

One consideration in the growing racism is the fact that the differentiation between Palestinians who are Israeli citizens and those who are in the Occupied Territories is very problematic and is the subject of debate within Israel. The Palestinians in the Occupied Territories have never received even formal civil rights, having been under straight occupation for the past nineteen years. Unlike the Palestinians who remained in Israel after 1948, they have several urban centres and a much more heterogeneous class structure. The occupation has affected social and economic relations within the West Bank, especially in terms of a growing dependency on Israel, as a supplier and consumer as well as an employer. But the most important effects of the occupation have been the emergence of a segregated Jewish settler society on lands confiscated from the Palestinians; a continuous military presence; deprivation of civil and legal rights; a continuously active resistance movement and a growing cycle of terrorization. The overwhelming majority of the Palestinians on the West Bank see their future in terms of an autonomous Palestinian state headed by the PLO – a political movement which has also gradually become more and more popular among Palestinians who are Israeli citizens, and who find themselves excluded from a future Palestinian state which would be in any way acceptable even to the most 'dovish' Zionists.

The Zionist 'doves', the Left of the Labour party, want Israel's withdrawal from most of the Occupied Territories and the establishment of a Palestinian state alongside Israel in these areas, thus keeping the Jewish character of the Israeli state without having to deviate too extremely from normal practices of western type democratic states. They would like to see the Israeli Palestinians as a small minority within Israel, with civil but no collective rights, and the bravest among them even talk about the eventual full assimilation of Israeli Palestinians into Israeli society.[29]

Such an assimilation, of course, negates not only the subjective feelings of most of the Palestinians in Israel, but also the fundamental existence of Israel as a Zionist state. It absolutely depends, as most of those who hold this position from within the Zionist camp admit, on the contiued existence of the Palestinians in Israel as a small minority. Hence a growing preoccupation with 'the demographic race' (as we shall see below).

However, the differentiation between Palestinians who are and those who are not Israeli citizens pales in significance next to the growing majority of Israelis who are claiming the Occupied Territories, especially the West Bank which includes the Jewish religious sites, as an exclusionary Jewish territory. From this position, the boundaries of Israeli civil society include not only Israel's citizens but also the inhabitants of the Occupied Territories, who constitute a third of the overall number of the Israeli population, and all of them are thus perceived as a threat. Containment, exploitation, oppression and ultimately expulsion are the various means suggested and used against the Palestinians, especially in the Occupied Territories. The aim is to include the territory but exclude its people from inclusion in the Israeli national boundaries.

The relationship between the Israeli national collectivity and the Jewish people has made its overall boundaries blurred and indefinite, and the criteria for 'membership' for 'Jews' in the collectivity open to both ideological and legal debate. The relationship with the Palestinians, both those who are Israeli citizens and those under its occupation, has opened a debate on the basic premises according to which the Israeli national collectivity will, in the long term, reproduce and defend its boundaries as a Jewish collectivity. Demographic policies stand at the heart of these debates and struggles.

PART II:
DEMOGRAPHIC POLICIES AND THE 'NEED'
FOR JEWISH MAJORITY

IN PART I of this article, I looked at the ways in which the boundaries of the Israeli Zionist national collectivity have been constructed. I examined the ambiguity of the Israeli Jews constituting themselves as a 'new' and separate collectivity from the Diaspora Jews but at the same time representing them in their state. I looked at internal ethnic and ideological divisions within Israel which have gradually and increasingly been challenging hegemonic conceptualizations about the nature of the Israeli society, especially during the last decade. And I raised questions deriving from a situation where non-Jews who are Israeli citizens and/or are living under Israeli control in territories claimed to be part of Israel, are at the same time being excluded from the Israeli national collectivity.

In this part of the article, I look at the implications that all these factors have had for demographic policies in Israel.

Basically these policies, although reflecting all the ambiguities, contradictions and tensions described above, have had two hegemonic goals:

--the first goal has been to maintain and if possible increase Jewish domination in Israel, both via the establishment of a numerical majority and via the pursuit of military and technological superiority over the Arabs;

--the second goal, which is increasingly occupying the minds of Israeli policy makers, has been to reproduce and enlarge the 'Jewish people' all over the world and to ensure that Israeli Jewish mothers produce enough children to 'compensate' for the children lost in the Nazi Holocaust and in what is called in Israel the 'Demographic Holocaust'.

Traditionally, as a settler society, immigration (*'aliyah*) was considered to be the quickest, as well as the cheapest and most efficient, method of increasing the Jewish Zionist presence in Palestine. Not that the specific composition of the Jewish immigrants was without its own internal contradictions. As the character of immigration changed from being predominantly young, single, ideologically motivated East Europeans, into bringing whole migrant communities with age compositions, ideologies and skills which were very different, so too the overall character of Israeli society changed. This demographic change took place many years before it began to challenge the Israeli power structure, as the later immigrants, mostly Oriental Jews, were tightly controlled by the Zionist institutions which were responsible for their absorption.

When we look at the demographic policies in Israel aimed at encouraging higher birth rates, we have to examine not only WHEN they were mostly introduced (which corresponded with the periods, overall, when outside sources of Jewish immigration were blocked), but also at the debates which developed in Israel concerning WHO should be encouraged to reproduce and HOW. To an extent there has also been the debate as to whether this question is at all in the domain of public debate, or whether it is an individual decision of the families involved, or even only of the women involved, as the small Israeli feminist movement has been claiming. The lack of clear policies concerning abortion, for example, up until the 1970s, has been just one symptom of the conflict between a liberal democratic ideology which saw decisions concerning child bearing as basically part of the private domain and an ideology which saw it as a patriotic duty. The change in the relative hegemony of each of these ideologies is but one symptom of the more general shift in dominant value systems in Israel. It is not a coincidence that when Efrat, The Committee for the Encouragement of a Jewish Birth Rate in Israel was first established in the 1960s, it was a bit of a public joke. Uri Avneri, for example, the editor of the weekly *Ha'olam Hazeh* which consistently supports civil rights in Israel, accused those who advocated this line of thought of having 'the psychology of rabbits'. But it is also not a coincidence that these days Uri Avneri himself writes editorials which explain the unavoidable need for a Jewish majority in Israel. [30]

The 'need' for a Jewish majority has always been a cornerstone of Zionist thinking, of which Avneri represents the most liberal wing. Ben-Gurion, debating in the Knesset in 1949 – during the war which expanded Israel's territory way beyond the territory allocated to it by the UN – explained: 'A Jewish state . . . even if only in the West of Palestine is impossible, if it is to be a democratic state, because the number of Arabs in the western part of Palestine is higher than that of the Jews . . . we want a Jewish state, even if not all over the country'. [31]

The Zionist strategic priority of a Jewish majority in Israel has been one of the issues debated all along between the Left and Right of the Zionist movement, especially before the state was actually established, and after 1967. In the time of the *yishuv*, the crucial thing for the Zionist Right, led by Zabotinsky, was Jewish sovereignty over the whole of Palestine. Once this could be established, it was assumed that the Jewish masses from all over the world would come and fill the country. The Labour Zionism that dominated the *yishuv*, on the other hand, saw Jewish settlement and a consolidation of a Jewish majority in a gradually expanding territory as a precondition for the establishment of the Zionist state. However, even they were prepared to accept a majority of only 55 per cent in the first instance, as was the situation in the planned Jewish state in the 1947 UN partition plan (which never actually materialized, due to the 1948 war), and planned various ways how to expand that majority. [32]

Plans for a transfer of the Palestinians outside the Zionist state have existed in more or less muted form throughout the history of Zionism, as one way of resolving the political contradiction of a Jewish state with too many non-Jews in it. During the 1948 war, Israel enlarged by more than 50 per cent its allocated territory, having divided the planned Palestinian state with Jordan. This could have meant a Jewish state with an over-whelming Palestinian majority. However, most of the Palestinians under Israeli rule either escaped during the battles and were never allowed to return, or were expelled by force. This, plus the major Jewish immigra-tion to Israel in the first few years of its existence from postwar Europe and from the Arab countries, had reduced the Palestinian minority in Israel in the early 1950s to no more than 11 per cent. Still, in the hope of reinforcing this ratio, Ben-Gurion initiated in the early 1950s rewards (of IL.100 – even then with more symbolic than substantial value) for 'heroine mothers' – i.e. those who have had ten children or more; he was continually calling on Israeli Jewish mothers to have more children.

The birthrates of the Jewish and the Palestinian populations within Israel were not, however, evenly balanced. In the early 1960s, there was, on the one hand, a halt in the mass Jewish immigration to Israel, and on the other hand the birthrate of the more traditionally oriented Israeli Jews began to fall. At the same time, the Palestinian birthrate in Israel did not decrease significantly, while their life expectancy increased (by 1967, the Arab minority in Israel constituted 15 per cent, in comparison with the 11 per cent of the early 1950s). A government committee was set up to review the demographic situation, as a result of which the Centre for Demography was established in 1967, and was attached to the prime minister's office (until 1978, when it became part of the government Work and Welfare Ministry) in order to develop suitable long term poli-cies to deal with the issue.

The 'ultimate threat' of the gradual growth of the Palestinian commu-nity in Israel and the erosion of the Jewish majority kept on growing as a political issue, especially after the 1967 war and the public debate about annexation of the Occupied Territories with their massive Palestinian population. But concern has also been growing in relation to the Palestin-ians who live within the 1949 borders, who are Israeli citizens, and who, for the first time in the last elections began to count, in sheer terms of numbers, as an important electoral lobby. [33]

This issue is central to the politics of Rabbi Kahane and others of his kind today-but not just to them. By 1976 it had already become a focus for widespread public paranoia in Israel, when a secret document written by Konig, the civil officer responsible for the Israeli Northern District, was leaked to the press. Galilee, with its concentration of Arab population, has always been a cause for concern to Israeli policy makers. In the mid-1960s, (before the 1967 war and around the time of the establishment of the demographic centre) major confiscations of Arab lands were carried out in Galilee, in order to establish in the heart of that dense Arab population, a new Jewish city, Karmiel. The official aim of this policy, initiated by Levy Eshkol, then prime minister, was to 'Judaize Galilee'. Konig expressed in the 1976 document his alarm that these policies had failed and that in the foreseeable future, the Arabs would constitute a majority in Galilee. Konig suggested various ways of combating this tendency, including settling Jews in areas densely populated by Arabs; encouraging Arabs to emigrate from the country by limiting their prospects of employment and studies, and cutting their child national insurance benefits and more. Since then, the 'demographic race' and the annual Jewish and Arab birthrate continue to be discussed prominently in the Israeli national press, accompanied with gloomy demographic predictions and/or attempts to refute them.

Israeli Palestinians have not necessarily been reluctant participants in the 'demographic race'. The fact of having large numbers of children, especially boys, has always been important in Arab rural society, which is organized around the extended family. It made possible a dignified existence for the old parents; it brought social honour to the mothers of sons; it also made possible a pooling of resoruces in times of economic hardship. The gradual proletarianization of the Israeli Palestinians was somewhat eased by the fact that while the men commuted to town to work, the women and other men of the family, stayed together in the village; in times of unemployment they constituted a buffer against its hardest effects. Nevertheless, gradually, especially with the rise of a new intelligentsia and the politicization of the younger generation, the authority of the *hamulas* (family clans), which the Israeli authorities have also cultivated as efficient means of control, has begun to diminish. In terms of population growth, however, modernization has had an immediate and contradictory effect-life expectancy has gone up; the mortality rate has come down; and together they have reversed the beginnings of a trend towards a falling birthrate.[34]

In addition, since the 1970s, family size has become a conscious political weapon among Palestinian nationalists. This has been true for the whole of the Palestinian movement. The training of children in refugee camps to be the next generation of fighters has been very central to it. War orphans, for example, have not been allowed to be adopted by outsiders (unlike Vietnamese orphans in similar circumstances), but are reared collectively for their national role. In Israel, the 'war on the baby front' became especially bitter in the 'post-Konig' period. Slogans like 'The Israelis beat us on the borders but we beat them in the bedrooms . . . ' started to be heard, and poems, a traditional mobilizing means in Arab societies, were written in this spirit. [35] The Israeli authorities more or less admitted that none of the active population control policies which are used in other Third World countries have any chance of meeting cooperation among either the 'traditional' or the 'modern' elements in the Arab sector. Nevertheless, social welfare clinics were set up, and Palestinian women are the only women in Israel who can obtain free contraceptives . . . I was told by a social worker that as long as these clinics were headed by Palestinian women, they tended to cooperate with the Israeli authorities on family planning policies (although from a very different motive to theirs – care for individual women rather than control of overall numbers). In the last few years Palestinian men have become heads of some of these clinics and it is rumoured that attitudes towards family planning have changed considerably.

Since the Israeli government is unable effectively to control the number of Palestinian children being born, quite a lot of its policies have concentrated on bringing in more Jews from abroad, and, when fewer and fewer actually came, at the same time gradually promoting and encouraging a growth of the Jewish birthrate in Israel itself.

After its establishment in 1967, the Demographic Centre commissioned coordinated studies on demographic trends in Israel and in the Jewish Diaspora, and promoted various pro-natal policies. This was done both by propaganda work and by material incentives, such as 'The Fund for Encouraging Birth' which was set up in 1968 by the Housing Ministry to subsidise housing loans for families with more than 3 children. These benefits, such as increased child allowances, were given basically only to Jews, under the euphemism of 'families who have relatives who have served in the Israeli army'.

Clearly the value of all these policies has been more symbolic than practical, when we take into consideration what is actually involved in bringing up a child. But even at this symbolic and auxiliary-practical level, these policies were not universally approved of in Israel.

One line of objection was raised by militant liberals and leftists. They joined the Israeli Palestinians in pointing out the racist character of using the state apparatus to discriminate against Palestinians and to block their access to a whole line of state benefits. Right-wing nationalists, however, also objected to using the state apparatus for that purpose – they would have preferred the Jewish Agency to take on this function. (As things stand, Palestinians who are Israeli citizens have been receiving some child benefit allowances, and the Druze and Bedouins who do military service have been even receiving the enlarged allowances that Jews receive. On the other hand, some Jewish families, especially among the extreme Orthodoxes, have no members of their family who have done national service; thus, under the euphemistic regulation, they have been entitled only to the reduced allowance. The Jewish Agency has in fact supplemented the allowances in such cases, first secretly and then openly; then, in the early 1980s, the Ministry of Religion began to take over this role.

Another line of argument against these policies was that, while promoting national goals, these policies do not take into account the class (and therefore also intra-Jewish ethnic) divisions in the Israeli society – inasmuch as it is the number of children rather than size of family income which is used as the qualifying criterion for child and housing benefits.

This line of opposition in the 1970s reflected a growing concern with issues of poverty and ethnic antagonism within the Jewish collectivity. Studies were published which showed that class differentiations between Ashkenazi and Oriental Jews in Israel had grown rather than shrunk in the course of the 1960s.[36] (This situation changed somewhat in the 1970s, due in large part to changes in the Israeli labour market after the influx of a large number of Palestinians from the Occupied Territories, and the consequent economic upward mobility of sections of the Oriental Jews. Nevertheless, the Jewish poor in Israel today are still overwhelmingly of Oriental origin.)[37]. Growing popular protest movements within what is often called 'The Second Israel' (the best known but by no means the only one being the Israeli Black Panthers) have brought this reality into the political arena as well, especially since the Oriental Jews have become a majority of the Israeli electorate.

The Government committee which was set up to examine these issues discovered an important and relevant fact. They found that, in Israel 75 per cent of children who grew up in Israel in economic deprivation come from large families of 4 + children, mostly from Oriental Jewish families, and that they constitute about 40 per cent of all Israeli children.[38] It pointed out the continuous and possibly growing class and ethnic divisions within the next generation of Israeli Jews, and also the shift in ratio between those belonging to the various different classes, as a result of the much larger number of children among people at the bottom end of the income bracket.

It is important to note in this context that although maintaining a Jewish majority in Israel has been a prime concern of the Zionist movement, Zionists are also always aware that in the Arab East it will always be a very small minority. The petty-bourgeois socio-economic background of most of the Zionist settlers before the establishment of the state; technological and organizational superiority over the underdeveloped Arab world; imperialist support of Israel as the most consistent local ally; and a nationalist myth of 'there is no alternative' – these are what has enabled the continuous success of Israel in its wars against the Arabs (at least until the Lebanon war). Quality, then, rather than quantity has been the crucial factor. (Over the last few years the situation has been changing, and Israeli newspapers report with anxiety that there is a much higher number of university graduates in the Arab world than in Israel; and, on the other hand, that there is a growing deterioration in the quality of the human material available to the Israeli army.[39])

It was therefore, again, primarily national concern, as well as an attempt to appease the growing protests of the 'Second Israel', which brought about a significant development in the direction of welfare policies in Israel in the 1970s – measures such as the introduction of social security, 'slum rehabilitation' programmes etc. For a while the (Jewish) family's economic situation, rather than the number of its children, became the official criterion for housing support.

This political trend, resulting from the fear of too many children growing up in poverty-stricken households in Israel, can also be said to be one of the major factors which, combined with ideological pressures, have brought about abortion legislation in Israel. For years there have been no official policies on the matter, because of politicians' fears of running into political trouble whatever decisions were taken.[40]

In fact, this legislation has become one of the major mobilization factors of the growing right-wing nationalist and religious camp. They see not only abortions, but also family planning in general and anything which results in families smaller than four children, as objectionable. Indeed, the secretary of the Efrat committee explained to me when I interviewed him that, since so many Israeli Jewish women get married and start bearing children only after completing their military service (at the age of twenty), any family planning aimed at limiting child-bearing to once every few years would necessarily severely limit the number of children such women could have before menopause.

For large sections of the pro-natal lobby in Israel, having many children is not just an inevitable outcome of keeping religious codes concerning procreation, or an expression of Jewish traditional values, or even a means of making Israel stronger by enlarging the number of potential soldiers. It is not even a question of keeping a Jewish majority in Israel. Having large families is seen as also a way of reproducing and enlarging the Jewish people which has dwindled, first as a result of the Nazi Holocaust (caused by anti-Semitism) and then by the 'Demographic Holocaust' (caused by assimilation and intermarriage). [41]

If, at the beginning of the Zionist endeavour, it was Jewish mothers in the Diaspora who produced human power for the *yishuv* settlement in Palestine, it was now the 'duty' of Israeli Jewish mothers to produce even more children for the sake of the Jewish people as a whole . . . In 1983, the Law on Families Blessed with Children was passed, giving a whole range of subsidies to families with more than 3 children.

The lobby which organized the pro-natal politics of the early 1980s revived the 'Efrat Committee for the Encouragement of Higher Jewish Birth rate' which had been dormant for most of the 1970s. In the 1980s, it became powerful enough to establish centres and branches all over the country and to incorporate in its ranks major elite figures from all professional fields, both religious and secular, and to gain official status as a governmental consultative body on natal and demographic policy committees (together with the official women's organizations).

A typical example of their advertisements which appeared in Israeli newspapers in Spring 1984 calls for Jewish families in Israel to have more children, because:

'As everybody knows, we are in a worrying demographic process. Doubly so – as there is more emigration and less immigration to Israel. The birthrate among the Jewish population in Israel is low. We are the sons of the Jewish people – we have to secure our future. For the sake of our first children, we have to bring into the world additional children. We have to enlarge our family frameworks in a significant and revolutionary way! It is a blessing and happiness in itself and will also bring about the saving of the Yishuv in the foreseeable future . . .' [42]

Among the many signatories to this advertisement are not only rabbis and religious intellectuals but also major figures from the Israeli medical and academic world, such as Professor Morris Levy, who won international fame as the first surgeon to carry out a heart transplant in Israel;

Professor Engelman of the Israeli Atomic Reactor at Soreq; and Professor Shavid, the head of the Department of Jewish Philosophy at the Hebrew University in Jerusalem.

Efrat gained a lot of its public power by linking the debate on encouragement of the Jewish birthrate to the public campaign around the abortion issue.

As part of its coalition agreement with the religious parties, the Begin government, when it came to power in the late 1970s, abolished the one category in the abortion law which enabled legal abortions to be carried out on the grounds of 'social hardship' (the other categories are: the woman's age; the pregnancy being a result of 'forbidden relations'; the health of the fetus and the health of the woman). This angered the feminist lobby but was not enough to appease the anti-abortion lobby, especially as liberal social workers on the abortion committees have tended to apply the woman's health category instead. [43] In addition to the usual reasoning of the anti-abortion lobby, who treat abortions as murder, came an emotive call to Jewish mothers to do their national duty and replace the Jewish children killed by the Nazis. An extreme (and narrowly defeated) example of this ideology was a suggestion by the then Advisor to the Minister of Health, Haim Sadan, to force every woman considering abortion to watch a slide show which would include, in addition to other horrors such as dead fetuses in rubbish bins, pictures of dead children in Nazi concentration camps . . . After a large public campaign this specific proposal was defeated and Sadan eventually resigned. Nevertheless, 'the war on the demographic war' continues.

It is worth remarking, however, that at the time of writing this article (winter 1985-6), the effects of the overall economic, political and ideological crisis in Israel, are making their mark on the various policies which have been used in the 'demographic race'. Within an overall context of drastic cuts in real wages and the threat of a rising unemployment, the effectively reduced state incentives have to a great extent lost any practical effects that they might have had a few years ago. This, plus a growing negative net migration to and from the country, have gradually and increasingly turned attention to the option of transferring Palestinians out of Israel, as the only possible valid long-term solution if Israel is to keep its Zionist character.

Still, on 6 January 1986, MP Avidov-Hacohen, of the Likkud party, suggested that 1987 be made an official year for 'the encouragement of Jewish birth rate in Israel'. Hooting and laughter greeted his speech in the Knesset, from the liberal and leftist benches, and wonderful satires followed in the press. But his suggestion received sufficient support for it not to be entirely defeated; it has been transferred for further discussion to one of the Knesset committees.

PART III
JEWISH WOMEN AND 'THE NATION'

WE HAVE SEEN how Israeli Jewish women have been 'recruited' in the 'demographic war' to bear more children, this being seen as their national duty to the Jewish people in general and to Israeli Jewish people in particular. It is debatable to what extent the ideological pressures, or the formal and material collective measures such as child benefits are the deciding influences in whether to have a child or, when an unplanned pregnancy occurs, to keep it. The emotional needs of people in a permanent war society, when husbands and sons might get killed at any moment, and cultural familial traditions probably play a more central role than anything else. Whatever the deciding factor, however, the fact is that Israeli Jewish women, especially professional middle class women, do tend to bear more children, than their counterparts in other advanced capitalist societies. [44] And their role as suppliers of children to 'the nation' has a direct effect on the availability of contraceptives and abortion. As I say, there are no free contraceptives in Israel except for Palestinians, and abortion legislation is a focus of major public political debates – not unique to Israel, but with a very explicit nationalistic emphasis, in comparison with campaigns in other countries where the 'Moral Right' has been fighting against abortion legislation.

Historically – until the 1960s, and since the beginning of the Zionist movement – it was mainly Jewish mothers in the Diaspora who 'supplied' the human power for the Zionist settlement to go forward. The Zionist endeavour can be described as an organization with clear international division of labour – in the Diaspora, the members and supporters of the movement supplied financial and political support and human power, and in Palestine, at the 'front', these resources were used to promote the Zionist project of imposing an exclusively Jewish society on Palestine. [45] This division of labour continues to date, and without the financial and political support of the Jewish Diaspora, Israel could not have continued to exist. In the supply of human material, however, the balance has gradually shifted and the discussions today focus, as we have seen, on the role of Israeli Jewish mothers in replacing the membership of the overall shrinking Jewish national collectivity all over the world rather than, or in addition to, the other way around.

Within the Zionist *yishuv* itself, the pressures on Israeli Jewish women to bear more children date from the beginning of the limitation on Jewish immigration to Palestine under the British mandate (I myself am a 'historical product' of Ben-Gurion's call for 'internal *'aliyah'* (immigration) in the early 1940s when the news of the Nazi Holocaust started to arrive . . .).

However, initially, as I suggested earlier, the main emphasis of Jewish motherhood in Israel was more to do with its qualitative aspect (of producing the 'New Jew' - 'the *sabra'* - the antithesis of the 'Diaspora Jew' whose negative image the Zionist movement shared with European anti-Semitism), rather than necessarily with quantity of children. The latter was seen as being fulfilled primarily via Jewish *aliyah* from abroad. The role of Israeli woman was to participate in the national struggle, mainly in supportive roles,[46] and, in addition, to produce proud, rooted and 'normal' children (whose characteristics would be 'earthiness', military strength, and, of course, the 'Jewish genius' . . .).

The development of the specific ideological construction of women as national reproducers in Israel has had a lot to do with the specificity of the historical development of the Israeli society as a permanent war society. The ideological placement of women in this respect was best summed up by MP Geula Cohen, a member of the neo-fascist Tehiyah party and an ex-member of the Stern gang in the pre-state period:

'The Israeli woman is an organic part of the family of the Jewish people and the female constitutes a practical symbol of that. But she is a wife and a mother in Israel, and therefore it is of her nature to be a soldier, a wife of a soldier, a sister of a soldier, a grandmother of a soldier. This is her reserve service. She is continually in military service.'[47]

There have been many myths concerning the role of Israeli women as soldiers (and I have expanded on it in another place.[48]). Basically, however, and to a great extent as in the civil labour market, women in the army serve in subordinate and supportive roles to that of men, unless they are in welfare and educational roles which directly correspond to the ideological tradition of women as mothers (rather than as wives and mistresses). The few women who are engaged in combative occupations are doing so in order to release men for front duties, from which women soldiers are officially banned. Also, as Geula Cohen says, women, unlike men, are released mostly from reserve service, which is the mass popular base of the Israeli army. Men serve at least one month a year in the reserves until they are fifty years old, and this is their most important national role. The women's national role then becomes to produce babies who would become soldiers in future wars. War widows (and parents) are perceived not only as people who have suffered the loss of their nearest and dearest, but as people who have made an active national contribution in their own right. It is on this basis that the value of war widows' compensations is set: they receive an income from the state, along with other privileges, all of which bears no relation to the income of the late husband before his death, and is comparable to a senior government office[49] (although, since the Lebanon war and the economic crisis, the real level of widows' income has been seriously eroded, as have most other Israeli state benefits).

This ideological construction can explain why groups like 'Women against the War' and 'Parents against Silence' have been so effective in their protest against the Lebanon war (together with Yesh Gvul, the first serious draft resistance movement in the history of Israel). They touched the heart of the ideological assumption that Israeli Jewish society is fighting only because 'there is no other alternative' if continuous collective survival is to be assured, and therefore the individual's sacrifices (constructed specifically according to gender and age and to a certain extent class and ethnic origin) are willingly made. When we look at the effects of the national reproductive role of Israeli Jewish women, however, it is important to remember that we are dealing here not only, and even not mainly, with effects which relate to the actual number of children they produce and for what. We are also concerned with the ideological and legal constraints within which this role of theirs is being constructed.

Jewish women in Israel, and for that matter in the Diaspora as well, are being incorporated actively in the Zionist endeavour, not only in supplying humanpower to the national collectivity, but also legally and symbolically, as markers of its boundaries. As I said in part I of this article, a Jew, according to the Law of Return, is somebody who was born to a Jewish mother (or is a religious convert). It is motherhood, therefore, rather than fatherhood that determines membership in the collectivity.

However, this matrilineal tradition does not mean, by any means, that Jewish society is a matriarchal one. It is not even fully matrilineal – since children take the family name of their father, not their mother. The adoption of collective matrilinearity as a means of determining who is a Jew was suitable in the context of the Jewish community as a persecuted minority, in which pogroms and rapes were historically a recurring phenomenon. In such a context, motherhood was a safer way of determining inclusive boundaries, and tight measures were taken in the religious code to secure the legitimate reproduction of the boundaries of the Jewish collectivity marked by its women.

Jewish women in the Diaspora can, in principle, choose whether or not to remain subjugated to the religious code. Not so Israeli women. The Israeli state apparatus has added its coercive power to the traditional voluntary Jewish communal power in several crucial instances, such as marriage and divorce, and gave it monopolistic rights.

Several attempts have been made since the establishment of the state of Israel to guarantee equal rights for women in terms of employment and payment, as well as protecting their rights as workers when they become mothers. This legislation suffers from limitations similar to other legislations found in this area in Western states, in which women are constituted in law primarily as wives and mothers. Another similarity with other countries is that this legislation fails to alter the basic segregation and inequality between women and men in the labour market. [50] What is more specific to Israel, however, is the fact that all attempts to guarantee women's overall equal constitutional rights in principle have failed. This has happened not so much as a result of direct intervention by the religious parties, but more by the preventive actions of the other Zionist parties, who feared that the religious parties would withdraw support from their coalition governments, and who also feared that any 'split of the people' would damage the Zionist claim to be 'the representatives of the Jewish people'. So, we have Rabin, the Labour prime minister in 1975 declaring that a Fundamental (= quasi constitutional) Law of Women's Equality would never be passed in Israel; moreover, already in the 1930s, at the height of the ideological zeal of the self-styled secular Labour Zionist movement, people were ready to give up women's right to vote, in order to prevent withdrawal of the extreme religious communities from the *yishuv* institutions (the Zionist settler community). What 'saved' the women then was the fact that the extremist religious parties withdrew anyway . . . [51]

Women do have the right to vote in Israel, although in recent years they have been prevented from doing so in local elections in some extreme religious settlements, especially among the settlers in the Occupied Territories (such as Immanuel). But in the 1950s, Golda Meir was prevented from becoming a candidate for the Mayorship of Tel-Aviv, because it was claimed that, according to the Halakha, women are not allowed to govern men'. (This position never changed; Golda was subsequently 'allowed' to become prime minister because, it was argued, her role there is formally that of 'first among equals' . . .

The most serious effects of the incorporation of religious laws into state legislation on women's status, relate to women's position in family law, where control of their constitution as bearers of the national collectivity is most carefully guarded. They are not allowed to become judges in the Orthodox Rabbinical state courts which have the decision-making monopoly in issues of marriage and divorce; furthermore, women's evidence, as a rule, is not accepted, especially if there are male witnesses. Questions of guardianship of children and maintenance are dealt with by two parallel court authorities – secular and religious; in the latter, most particularly, constructions of what should be the proper duties of a wife are exclusively decided by a small reactionary patriarchal group of Rabbinical judges. [56] (If she is proved not to have fulfilled them she is likely to be declared a 'rebel' and thus lose maintenance rights.) The inequality between the sexes also affects the women whose husbands disappear – in peacetime and even more so in Israel's continuous wars. Unlike men, women are not allowed to remarry until some proof can be brought that their husbands are in fact dead, and if they decide to live with another man and have children by him, the latter are declared as *mamzerim*, outcasts from the Jewish national collectivity for ever.

A Concluding Remark

WOMEN'S POSITION and women's roles, then, are thoroughly affected by Zionism's central concern for the reproduction of the Israeli national collectivity as Jewish. This article has examined some of the factors determining this relationship, and the series of debates which have accompanied various demographic policies that have attempted to reinforce it.

I began by quoting Rabbi Kahane when he stated that the issue of the Jewish character of Israel is the most central issue in Israeli politics – more important even than security. It is no coincidence, therefore, that the first proposal for a private member's bill that Kahane has raised in the Knesset related directly to the control of women's national reproductive role. He proposed to pass a law forbidding sexual relations between Jewish women and Arab men. (There have been reports in the press on the abuse that women who used to be married to Arabs suffer in the 'home' his organization has opened for them to move to[52]).

The Israeli parliament did not even have to reject Kahane's proposed bill, as legal means were found to prevent it from being formally introduced in the Knesset. (However, given the result for MP Avidov-Hacohen's proposal, one does wonder what would have happened if the proposal had actually been voted on . . .). Kahane, at least for the moment, in spite of (or perhaps because of) his meteoric rise in public popularity in Israel, is treated as an outcast in the Israeli Establishment, and there are even signs that his rising popularity has halted, with previous supporters shifting towards other right-wing parties like Tehiyah. I shall conclude my article, therefore, not with another quotation from Kahane (although he is very quotable) but from Uri Avneri, one of the most liberal of Israel's Zionists, an initiator of the Israeli-Palestinian Co-operation Committee and the Progressive List for Peace – the same Uri Avneri who mocked the 'rabbit psychology' of the demographic committees in the 1960s. In his editorial in *Haolam Hazeh* (24 April 1985) Avneri stated –

'The new Jewish community in this country, from the beginning of the Zionist *aliyah* until today, simply cannot absorb anybody who is not Jewish. One can argue "who is a Jew?". There are tensions between Ashkenazi and Oriental Jews, secular and religious, nationalists and humanists – but they all want to live in a state in which the Jews will live on their own, or almost on their own . . . If there is one people in the world who cannot absorb foreigners and keep an open bi-national, multi-religious society, it is the Jewish people . . . This is the real background for the historical debate on "territories for peace" . . . the only real choice is between a return to the [1949] borders of the state, within a framework of peace and co-existence, or a final deterioration into a Mediterranean South African state . . . '

I strongly reject the racist construction of the Jews by Avneri – after all, 75 per cent of contemporary world Jewry (who live outside Israel) do manage to live, and relatively happily at that, in ethnically diverse societies such as the USA and the Soviet Union. Indeed, some of them were among the strongest advocates for such societies. Nor do I accept this verdict as regards all the Israeli Jews who are engaged in anti-occupation struggles in Israel. However, it seems to me that this statement does signify the essence of the Jewish national collectivity that the Zionist movement is engaged in constructing and reproducing.

Is it the case that the dream of the Zionist-imagined community is in fact becoming a nightmare . . . ?

Notes

I would like to thank the members of the *Khamsin* editorial group, as well as Fouzi Al-Asmar, Debbie Bernstein, Uri Davis, Avishai Ehrlich, Ilana Ehrlich, Amira Gelblum, Miriam Kaini and Aliza Masarik for their helpful suggestions. Needless to say, the responsibility for what is actually written in this article rests solely with me.

1 Benedict Anderson, *Imagined Communities*, Verso, 1983.

2 Rabbi Meir Kahane, *Thorns in Your Eyes* (Hebrew), The Institute of Jewish Ideas, 1983, p9.

3 Quoted by Kahane, Ibid. p52.

4 Demographic Centre, *Goals and Means of Demographic Policy*, (Hebrew), Labour and Welfare Ministry, 1979.

5 See, for example, F. Edholm, O. Harris and K. Young, 'Conceptualizing Women', *Critique of Anthropology*. 3;9; O. Haris and M. Stivens, 'Women & Social Reproduction', unpublished paper; and M. McIntosh, 'Gender & Economics', in Young, Wolkowitz & McCullugh (eds.), *Of Marriage and the Market*, CSE Books, 1981.

6 See, for example, Sir William Beveridge, *Report on Social Insurance and Allied Services*, HMSO, 1942, p154:- 'With its present rate of reproduction, the British race cannot continue; means of reversing the recent course of birth rate must be found'. And in the Soviet Union, like in Israel they rewarded 'Heroine Mothers' for those with ten children and more. (*Guardian*, March 1979).

7 For further details on the initial reasons of the crisis see my paper, 'The current crisis in Israel' *Capital & Class*, no. 22, Spring 1984.

8 *The Scroll of Independence*, 14 May 1948.

9 For a summary of the main differences between the two tendencies, see Theodor Shanin, 'The price of suspension' in U. Davis, A. Mack & N. Yuval-Davis, *Israel and the Palestinians*, Ithaca Press, 1975.

10 A correction of the Knesset Fundamental (= quasi constitutional) Law no. 12, 1985.

11 See U. Davis, *Israel: Apartheid State*, Zed Books Ltd., 1987.

12 At this stage, the debate is not about using the religious definition itself, but whether or not conversions carried out by non-orthodox rabbis abroad should also be recognized.

13 See A. Leon, *The Jewish Question, a Marxist Interpretation*, Pathfinder Press, 1970; and I. Shahak, 'The Jewish religion and its attitude to non-Jews', *Khamsin* nos 8 & 9.

14 See my paper on 'Marxism and the Jewish Question', *History Workshop Journal*, October 1987 (forthcoming).

15 On the debate around this law see A. Orr, *The Unjewish State*, Ithaca Press 1983.

16 Reported in *Ma'ariv* (Israeli daily) 29 March 1984.

17 See *Davar* (Israeli daily) 6 May 1985.

18 S. Svirsky & D. Bernstein, 'Who worked in what, for whom and for what', (Hebrew) *Booklets for Research and Critique*, no. 4, 1980.

19 See the articles of Emmanuel Farjoun and Avishai Ehrlich in *Khamsin* no. 10.

20 *Fiddler on the Roof* is a famous musical based on the life of the East European Shtetl; 'Our village in the Atlas mountains' is a famous song by the Moroccan singer of the Natural Selection group.

21 'Sabra' is the nickname given to the Jews who were born in the *Yishuv* and in Israel. It is the name of a cactus which was widespread in Palestine. The Sabras are supposed to be like the fruit of the cactus–thorny on the outside and sweet inside . . .

22 There is still no good summary of this political trend in Israel although Maxim Ghilan tried to do it in his book *How Israel lost its Soul*, Penguin, 1974.

23 Masada is the name of the fortress mountain in the Judea desert in which the last rebels against the Romans resisted foreign rule to the end and committed

collective suicide rather than give themselves up to the enemy. It became a strong nationalist symbol of the Zionist revival; it is not incidental that Masada is also the nickname given to Israel's atom bomb . . .

24 An extreme example of the development of this political trend, focused around Gush Emunim and the settlers in the West Bank, is the way that the religious underground has been conspiring to bomb the Al Aqsa Mosque in order to be able to rebuild the Jewish Temple and bring about the advent of the Messiah.

25 *Israel Statistical Abstracts*, 1985.

26 See H. Rosenfeld, *They were Peasants* (Hebrew), Hotza'at Hakibutz Hame'uhad, 1964 and his later article in *Booklets for Research and Critique*, no. 3, 1978; see also S. Jiryis, *The Arabs in Israel*, Institute of Palestine Studies, 1968.

27 In the last elections there was an attempt to block The Progressive List for Peace, although it was an alliance between Palestinian nationalists and Israeli Jewish liberals and leftists; its Palestinian MP, M. Mi'ari had his parliamentary immunity taken away and there are all the signs that they will not be permitted to enter the next elections even in this format.

28 The press is every day full of new facets of anti Arab racism. To give just a couple of examples from the same week: the Chief Rabbi forbade Jews to sell their apartments to non Jews (*Ha'aretz* 17 January 1986) and survey results revealed that 42 per cent of Israeli Jews want the mass emigration of Palestinians from Israel (*Ha'aretz* 14 January 1986).

29 See, for example, the articles by Gershom Schoken, 'Ezra's Curse', *Ha'aretz*, 29 August 1985 and Yehoshua Porat, 'The state of the Jewish people or the Jewish state', *Ha'aretz*, 6 October 1985 (Hebrew).

30 Editorial in *Ha'olam Hazeh* (Hebrew), 24 April 1985.

31 *Protocols of the Knesset*, 4 April 1949.

32 See Y. Bailin, *The Price of Unification: the Israeli Labour Party until the Yom Kippur War*, (Hebrew), Revivim, 1985.

33 During the last election campaign, for the first time the election campaign by the major Zionist parties in the Arab sector in Israel did not take place mainly via traditional Hamula heads. This was especially true for the party headed by General Ezer Weizman.

34 Haim Ronen, 'Israeli Arabs multiply faster than the Chinese', *Bamakhane*, army weekly (Hebrew), 17 November 1982.

35 In May 1976, the poet Owani Sawit was arrested after reading some of his poems on the 'Day of the Land' memorial, including a poem in which he promised – 'Hey, murderers/ Do you really believe that you can murder my people?/ This is an impossible mission/ If you murder six, we shall bring to the world sixty on that same day' (Arabic).

36 S. Smooha, *Israel – Pluralism and Conflict*, RKP, 1978; see also the articles by S. Svirsky and D. Bernstien (Hebrew) in *Booklets for Research and Critique*, nos. 1 & 4.

37 See the articles by E. Farjoun and A. Ehrlich in *Khamsin* 10.

38 Report of the Prime Minister's Committee on *Children and Youth in Distress*, 1974 (Hebrew).

39 See, for example, Ari Sharit's article 'Is Israel withdrawing from the army?' (Hebrew) *Koteret Rashit*, 15 May 1985. Other similar articles appeared around that time also in *Ha'aretz* and *Ha'olam Hazeh*.

40 Y. Yishai, 'Abortion in Israel – social demand & political responses', *Policy Studies Journal*, vol. 7, no. 2 Winter 1978.

41 Professors Baki and Dela Pergulas of the Hebrew University are continually quoted in the press, predicting the shrinking of world Jewry from the present 11.5 million to 8 million by the year 2000 and to 5 by the year 2200, and pointing out that by now 43 per cent of world Jewry births are taking place in Israel (although less than 25 per cent of world Jewry actually live there).

42 Published in the Israeli press as an advertisement in June 1984.

43 The table in the *Efrat* bulletin (no. 15-16) shows that in 1979 there were 15,925 legal abortions in Israel, of which 1,665 were granted under the category of the age of the woman; 4,465 – forbidden relations; 2,165 – danger to the embryo; 1,299 – danger to the woman and 6,331 – the social situation of the woman; the last category was abolished in 1980 and in 1980 the number of abortions came down to 14,703. However, in 1982, the number of legal abortions was 16,829, 1,775 for age; 6,632 for forbidden relations; 2,626 – danger to the embryo; and 5,796 – danger to the woman. Clearly the last category has been used by the abortion committees as a substitute for the category which was abolished.

44 The average number of children to Jewish women in Israel in 1984 was 2.7, while it was less than 2, if not 1, in most western countries. For systematic comparison of the situation of women and the family in Israel and in other countries see Y. Peres and R. Katz, 'Family and Familiality in Israel', (Hebrew) *Megamot*, 26.1. pp 30-43.

45 See D. Hecht & N. Yuval-Davis 'Ideology without revolution: Jewish women in Israel' *Khamsin* 6 and A. Ehrlich, 'Zionism, demography and women's work', *Khamsin* 7.

46 See my booklet, *Israeli Women and Men: Divisions Behind the Unity*, Change publications 1982 and my article 'Front and Rear: The sexual division of labour in the Israeli army', *Feminist Studies*, vol. 11, no. 3, Fall 1985.

47 Geula Cohen, quoted in L. Hazelton, *Israeli Women – the Reality Behind the Myth* (Hebrew) Idanim, 1978.

48 See my article 'Front and Rear', op. cit.

49 L. Shamgar, *War Widows in Israeli Society*, (Hebrew), Ph.D. thesis, Hebrew University, 1979.

50 See, for example, Hilary Land, 'Sex role stereotyping in the social security and income tax system' in J. Chetwynd & O. Hartnett (eds.), *Sex Role Systems*, RKP, 1978 & Elizabeth Wilson, *Women and the Welfare State*, Tavistock publications, 1977.

51 Sarah Azaryahu, *The Organization of Hebrew Women for Equal Rights in the Land of Israel* (Hebrew), Keren leezrat ha'isha, 1977.

52 Reported in *Al-Hamishmar* daily, 27 February 1986.

Debbie Lerman

FEMINISM IN ISRAEL: A COMMON STRUGGLE?

THIS ARTICLE is an attempt to analyse, from an individual point of view, the lack of progress, difficulties and failures that have caused many women to discourage and abandon the perspective of a common struggle between Palestinian and Israeli women, in the context of the peace and anti-Zionist movement in Israel.

Countless hours of political action have been invested by women and men searching for correct and acceptable solutions to what is, for all practical purposes, virtually the stagnation of ideals of cooperation and solidarity between the Palestinian and Israeli left. This is not surprising, as the objective differences are so many that both sides sometimes stand beyond mutual comprehension, and thus make little progress in their attempts to reach mutually acceptable positions.

The main and most explosive difference is that of national identity, and the antagonism that is created when positions are seen or explained away as the result of conflicting national interests that are represented inside the movement.

Another major obstacle to cooperation has always been Zionism, its policies, and the day to day expressions of military occupation. Definitions and understandings of Zionism differ substantially between Palestinians and Israelis. Internationalism or anti-Zionism are not always an equalizer in this area.

A more insidious obstacle, and one which is hardly ever mentioned, is the racist attitudes and prejudices that exist among Israelis. Subtle or blatant expressions of racism on the Left and amongst feminists, colour every interchange between Jews and Arabs, despite the lip-service that is paid to condemnation of racism. Class differences, the result of decades of discriminatory and exploitative Zionist policies, are also a clear delineating factor. They account for patronizing attitudes and guilt on the part of the predominantly middle class, college educated, Ashkenazi Israeli progressives, and resentment on the part of the Palestinians, who are either working-class and peasant high school graduates, or first generation professionals fighting their way into a racist work market.

These schisms become even more pronounced when the analysis is adjusted to take account of the complex social stratification that results from the identification of individual Jewish people and communities as Ashkenazis or Sephardis; from the distinction as between populations that are urban or rural, religious or secular; from the division of people living under occupation pre- and post-1967 and from other divisive factors that are reflected in varying measures in the Palestinian or Israeli Left, and in the feminist movement. The resulting cultural differences that stem from social divisions, education, tradition and accepted patterns of behaviour, are the basis for many of the misunderstandings, especially when the factions attempting to cooperate are women.

Any common venture becomes very difficult due to the mismatch between the respective starting points of Palestinian and Israeli women. A woman's status in Israeli society is higher than that of her Palestinian counterpart, and so are the possibilities of social and political expression open to her. On the other hand, the majority of Palestinian women still live under the rule of a rigid patriarchy that deliberately hinders and delays their full integration in the social and economic development process that Palestinian society is undergoing. The Palestinian women that have changed their position are those active in the national struggle outside Israel, where concessions have been made by men as the price for women's contribution.

Zionism has supported and strengthened the traditional role of the family as a tool of conformity and repression. It has also helped women escape from patriarchy by introducing the capitalist mode of production into agrarian Palestinian society. The Israeli economy requires cheap labour for labour-intensive industries and agricultural settlements, and the demand is met by Palestinian women from the occupied territories and from Arab villages inside Israel. In this way they gain a limited measure of economic independence and a better education.

Another practical but very important obstacle to joint enterprises is the language barrier between Israeli women who do not speak Arabic, and the majority of Palestinian women who do not speak Hebrew or who are not willing to conduct a dialogue in the language of the invader. There are practical solutions to this problem, but it becomes a major headache when discussions are held by large numbers of women.

A further practical consideration that often defeats possibilities of joint activitiy is geographical segregation. Most Israeli activists live in predominantly Jewish towns. Most Palestinian activists live in areas where the population is almost exclusively Palestinian, both in the occupied territories and in villages and cities inside Israel (Acre, Jaffa, Umm al-Fahm). Thus any cooperation involving Palestinian women in the occupied territories meeting and working with Israeli or Palestinian women inside Israel, becomes a very dangerous enterprise that entails the risk of breaking military rules and suffering retaliation that bears no relationship to the political importance of the meetings attended. In general, the organization of any encounter, even if limited only to women living inside Israel, becomes a logistical nightmare.

The above has been a summary of the problems that have to be overcome in order to join forces and find a common ground. These differences between people's Palestinian and Israeli backgrounds exist, and they explain why the issues and strategies that concern people are also of a different nature. Actually, very few issues carry the same importance for both sides, precisely because of the reasons outlined above. Free abortion, contraception, claim back the night, pornography, careers, are areas of struggle that evoke little response among women that are more interested in mobilizing around ideas like day-care centres, basic education, community centres or job training. Nevertheless there are also many interests and problems held in common. Women are oppressed by men on both sides of the fence in the name of national needs and priorities; inside the movement, women's demands are put aside by more pressing issues such as national liberation struggle, organizing for socialist revolution or any activities against repression of civil and human rights. The longstanding national confrontation has validated and hardened male values that become the socially accepted mores.

Palestinian women outside Israel and Israeli women are excluded from the war-games and become supporting characters to men playing roles of machos, warriors, protectors, heroes. The atmosphere of war, violence and intolerance is not an ideal environment in which women can thrive, and the stereotypes perpetuate their status as outsiders to the mainstream.

This outlook is aggravated by powerful currents of religious fanaticism and fundamentalism, that have become a real danger to women, in both their political and their social expressions.

In order to survive and protect the small progress made on both sides of the fence, cooperation and solidarity between women is a very important tool. In practice, feminists and socialist feminists that endorse these views have been involved in several attempts to put this into practice. These attempts are channeled into three basic alternative options: joint Israeli-Palestinian groups; feminist organizations; or involvement in the political activism of the peace movement, socialist organizations or anti-Zionist groups.

The best examples of the first kind are groups like Women Against the Invasion of Lebanon, Women Against Occupation, Women's Committee of the Progressive List for Peace, etc. In these groups, Israeli and Palestinian women found a common ground on which a joint enterprise could be undertaken. Women Against the Invasion of Lebanon and its sequel, Women Against Occupation were joint enterprises of Palestinian and Israeli members of the Communist Party, the anti-Zionist left and the feminist movement. Outraged by the invasion of Lebanon, they organized around a loose platform that principally voiced their protest against the war. Later the group broadened its target to include Zionism and its policies, especially as they affect women. Its main activities were a series of demonstrations and publications directed mainly to women, adding the feminist perspective to anti-Zionist activities.

The women's committee within the Progressive List for Peace was started by the socialist feminist women in the List, and based its activities on a draft platform of agreed items and compromises reached by the organization's Israeli and Palestinian components. The committee ran candidates in the Naamat and Histadrut elections, and published papers on a number of issues. This kind of feminist activism, as can be seen from the above examples, is expressed in sporadic ad hoc projects related to current events, to outstanding atrocities, to the pet idea of one individual or to the short-lived actions of a particular group.

Such groups work reasonably well for the duration of their existence, although their political clout and their radius of influence never reach beyond the periphery of feminist and leftist supporters. So their main achievement is the mere fact of their being a joint effort, and a series of publicity-oriented actions.

The second alternative open to women is political activism in any of the

the peace, socialist or anti-Zionist organizations, whose work is consistently carried out with hardly any feminist considerations. There, feminists support political platforms that, except for token concessions, ignore feminist theory and disregard women as subjects of political interest. When attending exclusively to women's issues, most of the feminist involvement of women is among their peers. In that case, the central issues are limited to issues which interest that specific group of women – Palestinians or Israelis. Obviously, different objectives might be preferred if the choice was made with a common action in sight.

The question is, which alternative is the optimal choice?

Political activism in the midst of your peers is, at least in theory, easier and more productive. It is also true, in theory, that it is better to join the forces of women trying to reconcile the national and feminist angles.

In my opinion, the answer is not a clear cut choice but a selective combination of options that take into account the constantly changing situation, the limited number of women involved and the importance of showing that cooperation is a viable option. It is imperative, although beyond the scope of this article, to find new ways to match today's priorities, as it seems that the old and well used tactics and strategies, which never applied fully to this political environment, are now obsolete. The definition of new strategies is a *sine qua non* if any significant progress is to be made.

Our efforts in this direction are best channelled not to the top issues of the day as defined by the media, but to the basic matters that affect women and their lives. This approach might also be better understood and accepted by non-political women.

Limited goals are better suited to limited possibilities. The operative conclusion is that plans and strategies should aim for long term perspectives, built around basic questions that can be approached by any group. Palestinian and Israeli men have opened channels of dialogue with interesting and positive perspectives that feminists must learn to use.

We should also make better use of the lessons that have been learned by many women in a trial and error process that has been going on in many other parts of the world.

The main precondition is that the dialogue is kept open, allowing the interchange of information in meetings, in writing, by the creation of networks and such like. Hopefully these means will, in due course, become the seed from which a feminist Palestinian-Israeli movement will grow.

Note to the reader

Readers who have encountered Khamsin in the past, will have noticed some changes in the format of our latest issue. For them, as well as for those of our readers who encounter Khamsin for the first time, we would like to provide a brief history of our project and its aims, to explain the recent changes that this publication has undergone and our plans for the future. We are hoping to actively involve those of our readers who take a keen interest in a socialist future for the Middle East, in the ongoing debate on this issue.

Khamsin was established in 1975 as a French language journal in order to create a common forum for socialists in the Middle East from both the Arab world and Israel. Its initial concern was the struggle for basic democratic and national rights of the Palestinian people from a socialist perspective.

Based in London as an English language publication since 1977, it has taken up the much wider perspective of the Middle East as a whole. Written mostly by people from the area, it attempts to provide a thorough analysis of the economic, political and cultural problems facing the various classes.

As in the past, Khamsin is a publication by and for revolutionary socialists of the Middle East, as well as for socialists in other countries who are interested in that part of the world.

Khamsin is a committed publication. It aims not merely to reflect and express, but also to be part of the struggles for social liberation and against nationalist and religious mystifications.

All these struggles:

● That of the Arab popular masses against imperialism, Zionism and the Arab ruling classes;

● That of the Palestinian people, the most direct victims of Zionism, against their national and social oppression;

● That of the anti-Zionist left inside Israel;

● That of the labouring classes in all the countries of the Middle East against 'their own' exploiters, and against oppressive class regimes throughout the region;

● That of women throughout the region against their oppression and exploitation as women.

All these are inseparable aspects of one struggle, whose goals can only be achieved through the revolutionary overthrow of imperialist domination, the Zionist power-structure and all the existing regimes in the region, and the establishment of a united socialist Arab world, within which the non-Arab nationalities will also enjoy, by right and in fact, full social equality, individual liberty and national freedom.

The members of Khamsin collective, from various countries of the region and belonging to different political tendencies, are united round this aim. However, Khamsin is not a political organ but a forum in which aims themselves, as well as the strategy for achieving them, can be debated and discussed among the various shades of revolutionary left opinion.

While maintaining the same political perspective and aims, Khamsin has recently undergone several structural changes:

Khamsin is published from now on by Zed Books. For this, and related technical reasons, Khamsin has been transformed from a journal into a book series. Apart from changing format, the above transformation also means that each issue of Khamsin will contain from now on a number of articles wholly dedicated to a single topic, rather than a main theme accompanied by articles related to other topics as before. For this reason, we will no longer be able to include readers' letters and debates carried on from previous issues in the Khamsin book itself.

This is not to say that our commitment to providing a socialist debate forum on the Middle East has in any way weakened. Quite the opposite:

While the Khamsin books will continue to provide thorough and analytical articles, we now intend to produce a parallel forum for discussion and debate, which will be circulated amongst all those who wish to take part in it.

Being published more frequently that the Khamsin books, this forum will be able to provide a more topical discussion on current Middle Eastern affairs, selections from Arab and Israeli press, reviews of publications on the Middle East, resonses to material published in the Khamsin books and the Khamin forum themselves or in any other publication on the Middle East.

The success of this new Khamsin project largely depends on you, our reader, whatever your country of residence may be. Please write to our address below, indicating your wish to receive the Khamsin bulletin regularly (you don't have to be a subscriber to the Khamsin books series for that). You are also welcome to send us your comments, reviews and short articles.

Yours comradely
Khamsin collective
B.M. Khamsin
London WC1N 3XX
U.K.

Khamsin

A publication of revolutionary socialists of the Middle East.

Editorial Group: Haim Bresheeth, Alain Hertzmann, Hamida Kazi, Daniel Machover, Moshé Machover, Ani Manoukian, Sonia al-Nimr, 'Adel Samara, Haim Scortariu, Nira Yural-Davis.

☐ **Khamsin Collective:** Dan Diner, Avishai Erlich, Emmanuel Farjoun, Alexander Flores, Dina Hecht, Muhammad Ja'far, Leila Kadi, Lafif Lakhdar, Mario Offenberg, John Rothschild, Magida Salman, Azar Tabari, Khalil To'ama.

Articles and editorial correspondence: send to *Khamsin*, BM *Khamsin*, London WC1N 3XX, UK. Authors are asked to send in two copies of their typescript, typed on A4 sheets (297mm × 210mm) with broad margins and not more than thirty lines per page.

Back issues:
- *Khamsin 5*, **Oriental Jewry**, £3.50 (USA. $5.00) each.
- *Khamsin 6*, **Women in the Arab World**, out of print.
- *Khamsin 7*, **Communist Parties of the Middle East**, £3.50 (USA. $5.00) each.
- *Khamsin 8*, **Politics of Religion in the Middle East**, £3.50 (USA. $5.00) each.
- *Khamsin 9*, **Politics of Religion/Capitalism in Egypt**, £3.50 (USA $5.00) each.
- *Khamsin 10*, **Israel and its War in Lebanon**, £3.50 (USA $5.00) each.
- *Khamsin 11*, **Modern Turkey: Development and Crisis**, £3.50 (USA $5.00) each.
- *Khamsin 12*, **The Gulf War/Arab Nationalism and the Palestinian Struggle**, £3.50 (USA $5.00) each.

☐ **Back issues** and single copies to individuals available from bookshops and direct from *Khamsin*, BM *Khamsin*, London WC1N 3XX, UK. Mail, add 50p p&p. If paying by cheque drawn on a bank outside UK, add £1.00 handling charge.

☐ **Subscriptions:** individuals £12 (USA $22), institutions £17 (USA $32), postfree, for three issues. If paying by cheque drawn on a bank outside UK, add £1.00 handling charge.

☐ All cheques etc. to be made payable to *Khamsin*, and sent to BM *Khamsin*, London WC1N 3XX, UK.

☐ **Bookshop orders** and sales enquiries to Zed Books, 57 Caledonian Road, London N1, UK. Telephone 01-837 4014/0384.